Messiah and His Hebrew Alphabet

Studies in the Hebrew Alphabet
With Messianic Overtones From
Aleph — The Sacrifice
to
Tav — The Cross

Dick Mills and David Michael

Dick Mills Ministries
Orange, California

Unless otherwise indicated, scripture references are from the *King James Verion* as paraphrased by the authors.

Messiah and His Hebrew Alphabet
Published by:
Dick Mills Ministries
P.O. Box 2600
Orange, CA 92669
ISBN 0-9629011-1-3

Second Printing, May 1996

Editorial Consultant: Phyllis Mackall

Cover design and book production by:
DB & Associates Design Group, Inc.
P.O. Box 52756, Tulsa, OK 74152

Printed in the United States of America.

"I am the first, and I am the last...."
—Isaiah 44:6

"I am Aleph and Tav, the Beginning and the End, the First and the Last."
—Revelation 22:13 *Hebrew New Testament*

Contents

Foreword

The essence of Bible study, and, thereby, spiritual growth. is to grasp and receive *the spirit of the Word.*

Every study resource that assists the penetration of the spirit *behind* the words which comprise the Holy Scriptures is worthy of commendation and use. And on the grounds of study alone, I heartily encourage your pursuit of searching God's Word — the Bible — aided by this product of the scholarship of Dick Mills and David Michael.

But those grounds are enhanced by even more preferred terrain — the goal of growth. For since the true spirit behind all words in the scriptures is the Holy Spirit, to imbibe the Word more deeply is to drink of Him. And to so fill yourself is to become more filled with and more like Jesus Himself.

So study — and drink to the full. The words (and the letters) of the Word are components to spiritual blessing, purity, and power.

Jack Hayford, Pastor
The Church on the Way
Van Nuys, California

Introduction

The Hebrew alphabet has a great fascination and stimulating interest to Christian believers. Each of the 22 letters in the alphabet has a message with Messianic overtones.

The purpose of this book is to look at each letter, give its basic definition, and point out the Messianic import each letter shows.

Antiquity reveals early writing to be pictures, symbols, and hieroglyphics. As time passed, picture-words became word-pictures. Letters had symbolic value and definitions. Although the Greek alphabet does not have definitions, the Hebrew alphabet, being older and linked with pictures, does contain letters that can be defined.

From the first letter, *aleph*, the sacrificial animal, to the last letter, *tav*, the cross, it is easy to see the Messiah in each of the letters!

Another note of interest is the triad tendency of the Hebrew language. Of the 6,043 regular words that make up the Hebrew and Chaldee Old Testament, 3,491 (nearly 60 percent) are three-letter words.

A good question to ask language experts would be, "Why is this one language made up predominately of three-letter words? No other language shows this tendency. Why the Hebrew triads?"

It was said of Matthew Henry that everywhere he looked, he could see the Messiah centered in his observations. We are not trying to read something into the Hebrew alphabet that is not there, but the three-letter word structure to the Christian is a reminder of the Trinity.

It is easy for a believer to see the similarities between the Father, Son, and Holy Spirit and a religious language that is mainly comprised of three-letter words. Some Bible scholars have suggested that Zephaniah 3:9 could refer to the Hebrew language; for example, "In that day the peoples of earth will speak one common language" (Andrew Edington, *The Word Made Flesh*, 1975, John Knox Press).

The thought is that Messiah will set up His kingdom on the Earth. He will undo the effects of the language confusion at the Tower of Babel. All the languages of the Earth will then be changed to one universal language!

The Living Bible says of Zephaniah 3:9, "At that time I will change the speech of my returning people to pure Hebrew so that all can worship the Lord together."

One of the fascinations of the Hebrew language is its religious focus. Most of the other languages in the world were developed and set in military, political, or commercial surroundings. For example, Alexander the Great conquered nations and converted their languages to Koine Greek. Thus, military conquests determined the language of a nation.

In the case of the Hebrews, military, political, and commercial factors were secondary to the people and their worship. As this language developed, it gave the people a vehicle of expression in worship, teaching the *Torah*, learning the statues, and becoming acquainted with the ways of the Lord. To structure a language around a people's worship and religious service sets that language apart and gives it a distinction no other language has.

Owen C. Whitehouse in *The Century Bible* comments on Isaiah 44:6 ("I am the first, and I am the last"), "The significant expression, 'the first and the last' passed into apocalyptic language. In the final utterance of the Book of Revelation, it is assumed by Jesus as one of His own divine titles" (Revelation 22:13).

Could it be that "I am the first, and I am the last," as recorded by Isaiah 44:6, could include the Hebrew alphabet? The statement "I am *aleph*, and I am *tav*" would coincide with the New Testament statement of Jesus, "I am Alpha and Omega, the beginning and the end, the first and the last" (Revelation 22:13).

Jesus ties both testaments together with this statement for New Testament believers: "I am the first and last letters of the alphabet, *Alpha* and *Omega*. For the Old Testament believers I am *aleph* and *tav*, the first and the last." Because of this statement, it is easy for us to see Jesus alluded to in every letter of the Hebrew alphabet!

We want you to familiarize yourself with each letter in the Hebrew alphabet. If you are a Christian believer, we pray you will be spiritually edified and encouraged to see Jesus in every letter of the alphabet.

If you are a Messianic Jew, we pray *shalom v'berachot* (peace and blessings) for you. We believe you will see *Yeshua*, the Messiah, in every letter.

If you are Jewish and looking for *emet* (truth), we pray this book will speak *al lev* (to your heart).

The word studies in this book were compiled by Dick Mills and the devotional comments by David Michael.

Dick Mills

Dick Mills
Hemet, California

(Pronounced AW-LEF)

Chapter 1
Aleph: **The Sacrificial Animal**

Technical Data: 871 words in the Hebrew Bible start with *aleph.* Of these, 374 are proper names and places, and 497 are regular words. The Greek equivalent of *aleph* is *alpha.*

Aleph is the first of two Hebrew letters which have no equivalent English sound. *Aleph* is simply the breathing enunciated with a number of vowel sounds with which the letter is connected.

It would be easy to assume that *aleph,* which commences the Hebrew alphabet, as *alpha* does the Greek, should be equivalent to the letter "a," but this is not necessarily the case.

Jewish Definitions: Jewish writers state that *aleph* denotes abundance and strength, referring to Psalm 144:14, "Our oxen *[aleph]* are heavily laden" (*Wisdom in the Hebrew Alphabet,* page 51). Some writers also state, "The shape of an *aleph* in the ancient script resembles an ox-head."

Christian Definitions: The very first letter of the Hebrew alphabet draws attention to the sacrificial system of blood sacrifice as practiced by Israel.

Hastings' *Bible Dictionary* says *aleph* is "An ox — from the resemblance of the letter to the front view of the head and horns of that animal." *Gesenius' Hebrew and Chaldee Lexicon* refers *aleph* to *alluph*, a tame, docile, gentle lamb or bullock. John MacMillan states in *Christ in the Hebrew Alphabet*, "Aleph is the animal ready for service and ready for sacrifice."

Devotional Comments

Aleph comes from the word *alluph*, meaning "an ox or bullock." The word *alluph* itself also carries the suggestion of being "gentle, tame, familiar, and friendly." The first thing that an ox suggests to us is strength. People often use the phrase "strong as an ox."

Throughout history it has been oxen which have plowed our fields, and, when yoked together in greater numbers, pulled our heavy loads. When an ox reaches a certain degree of strength, it begins to serve as a worker.

Oxen or bullocks were among the kinds of animals which were acceptable as sin offerings, according to the laws concerning sacrifice. (See Leviticus 4:1-21.) The only animals which could be sacrificed at all were those considered clean, or, in other words, those whose flesh is *kosher*. This included sheep, goats, bullocks or oxen, doves, and pigeons.

In addition to belonging to one of the clean meat species, the animal had to be "without blemish." In Hebrew it is *tamim*, meaning "perfect." So the biblical picture that the ox portrays is one of a clean animal, strong enough to serve and capable of being sacrificed.

We see a beautiful illustration of the various uses for oxen in the account of the call of Elisha in First Kings 19:19-21. Elijah found Elisha plowing with twelve yoke of oxen. Elisha determined to leave his family and follow Elijah, so he immediately took some of the working oxen, butchered them, and served the meat to his family as a farewell dinner. Even the wooden yokes with which the oxen had been plowing were used to make the fire for cooking.

Another good example is the account of the Ark of the Covenant returning to Zion (2 Samuel 6). The Ark was put on a new cart which was pulled by oxen. When the Ark came to rest in Jerusalem, it was oxen that were sacrificed, and thus began the great celebration in which David danced spectacularly. Again, it was oxen that served as *laborers* and then as *sacrifices*.

We read in the New Testament a beautiful scripture which describes Jesus as a youth: "And the child grew, and waxed strong in spirit, filled with wisdom: and the grace of God was upon him" (Luke 2:40).

This verse explains that Jesus grew strong in His childhood and prepared Himself for a life of *service*. During the years of His ministry, He labored hard in His Father's vineyard and showed us the pattern of service to God.

How numerous were the times He was faced with multitudes of sick people needing to be healed, "...and he healed them *all*." (See Matthew 12:15; 15:30; Mark 6:31-44; Luke 4:40; 6:19.) Jesus said of Himself that He came to *serve*, not to be served (Matthew 20:28).

It was during these strenuous years of service that He was also preparing to be *sacrificed*. Jesus plainly spoke of His death before it happened, and He made it clear that no one was going to take His life from Him, but that He was going to lay His life down voluntarily as a ransom for sinners (John 10:17,18).

What do we see in *aleph*? We see the strength of this sacrificial animal, its life of hard work, and its sacrificial death. This letter *aleph* points to the life, ministry, and death of Jesus!

(Pronounced BET)

Chapter 2
Beth: **The House**

Technical Data: 469 words in the Hebrew Bible start with the letter *beth.* Of these, 212 are proper names and places, while 257 are regular words.

The *beth* (house) words make up the majority of proper names; 49 *beth* words occur, ranging from *Beth-Aven* to *Beth-Tappuah.* Next in frequency are the *baal* (master) words. The range from *Baal-Berith* to *Baal-Tamar* totals 15 *baal* words. Third in frequency is *ben* (son). Twelve *ben* words occur, from *Ben-Oni* to *Ben-Ammi. Beth* in the Greek alphabet is *beta.* Our English letter is "b."

Jewish Definitions: Jewish writers concur that *beth* means "house," and add that the word alludes to the focal point of holiness on Earth, or the house of God being the meeting place of a holy God and His people.

Christian Definitions: Beth means "house, tent, or family." Originally, the letter *beth* was squared and had the outline of a house. The very word "house" has much significance. *Beth-el* is "house of God." *Bethlehem* is "house of bread." Jesus the Bread of Life was born in Bethlehem!

Devotional Comments

The second Hebrew letter, *beth,* represents a house. Its shape even today suggests a house or a cottage. As a matter of interest, the word *beth* itself means "house" in Hebrew.

In English we do not have words that mean the same thing as individual letters. For example, we would not use the letter "c" to represent a sea. The closest we come to this concept in our language is in such phrases as "A-frame house," "T-bone steak," "at the Y in the road," and so forth, where an object assumes a name because it is shaped like one of our 26 letters.

There will be other instances where the name of the Hebrew letter is equal to the word for the item that the letter represents, and these cases will usually be noted as we examine each letter.

The word *beth* (house) can be pronounced two ways — *beyt* or *bah-yeet* — both spelled with the same three Hebrew letters. Generally it is *beyt* when it is part of a place name like *Beth-Shemesh* (house of the sun).

Elsewhere, it is *bayit,* which means "house" in the widest sense of the word: house as in building; house as in the family or household — for example, the house of Aaron, the house of Saul, the house of David; house as in tribe or nation — for example, the house of Judah, the house of Israel; and house as in Temple — the house of the Lord.

This word *beyt* (or *bayit)* is one of the most important words in the Hebrew language, covering the idea of house, home, family, tribe, nation, and temple.

There were many references to houses in Jesus' life and ministry. His first miracle was performed at a wedding — the beginning of a new household. He went into the home of a notorious sinner, and the man was so greatly changed that Jesus could say, "This day is salvation come to his house."

He told a parable about two houses, one built on rock and the other built on sand. He referred to His physical body as a "temple" or a "house." He referred to the human body in general as a "house" which could be inhabited (Matthew 12:43-45).

The Hebrew word for "synagogue" is *beyt-knesset*, which means "house of gathering." We read in Matthew 9:35 that Jesus went about all the cities and villages, teaching in their synagogues and preaching the Gospel of the kingdom and healing every sickness and every disease among the people.

The scripture also tells us that it was Jesus' custom to read the scriptures publicly in His hometown synagogue in Nazareth. But there was a greater "house" where He spoke on many occasions, and that was the Temple in Jerusalem.

It was in the courts outside the building where the people congregated, and it was in these courts where Jesus frequently taught. The whole Temple compound is atop Mount Moriah and is called *har ha-bayit* (mount of the house), or as we say, "the Temple Mount."

Jesus first visited the Temple Mount when He was six weeks old, as His parents went to Jerusalem to fulfill the requirements of the Law of Moses concerning a woman's purification after giving birth. (See Luke 2:21-39.) This rite, and the specified sacrifice connected with it, is described in Leviticus 12:1-8.

While at the Temple for the sake of this offering, Jesus and His parents were approached by Simeon, a devout citizen of Jerusalem. Simeon, taking the infant Jesus up in his arms, uttered a dramatic prophecy of destiny over the child: "Behold, this child is set for the fall and rising again of many in Israel; and for a sign which shall be spoken against...that the thoughts of many hearts may be revealed" (Luke 2:34,35).

This child, over whom a nation could fall, and through whom the nation would rise up again, was called by Simeon "the glory of your people Israel," "a light to enlighten the Gentiles," and even "the salvation of the Lord." This word "salvation" is *Yeshua* in Hebrew, and *Yeshua* is also the Hebrew name by which our Lord was called (which in English becomes "Jesus").

It was also here at the Temple that Jesus at age 12 was found reasoning with the scholars of the Law. Here He came every year with His parents for Passover (Luke 2:41).

At Hanukkah, Jesus was walking through Solomon's Porch at the Temple when a great controversy occurred over His teaching (John 10:22-40).

It was at the Temple during Hoshanah Rabbah (the Great Hosannah) on the final day of Succot (Tabernacles) that Jesus proclaimed His message of life-giving water (John 7:37-39).

It was at the Temple that Jesus resolved the highly explosive issue of the woman who was caught in adultery (John 8:3-9). Here also He commended the widow who put into the Temple treasury a small offering, which was all the money she possessed.

The most famous incident concerning Jesus at the Temple was when He drove out the sellers of animals and the moneychangers during the Passover season (John 2:13-23).

He revealed His intimate relationship with the Almighty in His warning to the merchants in the Temple: "Do not make *my* Father's house a house of merchandise!" He reminded them that it was written that God's house shall be a house of prayer for all people. So many New Testament events occurred at the Temple, we cannot refer to all of them in this short study.

The Book of Hebrews tells us that Moses was a faithful servant in his house, and that Jesus is the Heir of the house which we belong to if we are faithful.

Jesus labored to prepare a place for us in His Father's household. Jesus was God's tabernacle among men — *Immanuel*, meaning "God with us." He also speaks of the future, when the tabernacle of God will come down from heaven and dwell among men forever. This is the glorious future of Messiah's kingdom.

Because Jesus spent His life on Earth laboring to secure such a place for others, He did not put any value on obtaining a house for Himself. He said, "The Son of man has no place to lay His head" (Luke 9:58). That was the pattern through much of His life.

He was not born in a house; He was born in a stable. During the time Jesus resided in Capernaum (perhaps two years), He lived in the home of Peter and his wife and her mother. When Jesus was buried, it was in a tomb that a compassionate member of the Sanhedrin donated.

So in birth, in life, and in death it was the same: The Heir, Builder, and Purifier of God's house did not seek a material home for Himself.

Beth points to the Messiah, who personally is the House of the Lord God!

(Pronounced GIM-MEL)

Chapter 3
Gimel: **The Burden Bearer**

Technical Data: There are 327 Hebrew words in the Old Testament that begin with the letter *gimel*. Of these, 102 are proper names and places, and 225 are regular words. The Greek equivalent of *gimel* is *gamma*. Our English letter is "g."

Jewish Definitions: Jewish writers compare *gimel* with *gamol* ("to nourish until completely ripe"), adding that the shape of the letter *gimel* resembles a camel with its long neck. The camel received its name because it is like a weaned child. It can go for a long time without drinking.

Christian Definitions: James Strong defines *gimel* as the camel in the sense of burden bearing. John MacMillan defines *gimel* as the camel associated with travel, burden bearing, and endurance. John Montgomerie likens *gimel* to the camel and a lonely journey. James Hastings defines *gimel* as "a camel that is recumbent."

Devotional Comments

The third letter, *gimel*, represents a camel. The word "camel" in Hebrews is *gamal*. The word *gamal* also means "to

11

do good, to benefit," and, in other Semitic languages, "to carry." This portrays the abundance of services which the camel provides.

Most people know that the camel has been called "the ship of the desert," and that camels are suited to travel great distances over trackless land. Fewer people are aware that travel by camels is considered the original method of human transportation, predating travel by horses, ships, litters, or chariots.

The camel's utility and worth were evidently appreciated by the entire ancient world, because the word *gamal*, or camel, is found throughout all the Phoenician and Semitic languages, as well as in Greek, Latin, Old Egyptian, and Sanskrit (where it appears in the form *kramela*).

We read in Genesis 31:17,18 that the patriarch Jacob's wives and sons traveled great distances on camels. Travel by camel was practiced in some degree from Bible times to the present day. This shows that for many societies the camel has been a useful burden bearer.

The camel is legendary for its ability to exist comfortably without water for extended periods of time. This is made possible through certain aspects of the camel's physical characteristics.

Two factors in particular are the ability of the animal to store fluid in its excess body fat and the special water storage cells in its stomach which seal off when filled. Thus, the camel has an internal supply of stored water which can be continuously released as needed, and this makes it completely independent of its dry environment.

This factor immediately reminds us of the introductory sentences of Isaiah 53, the chapter which speaks of God's Suffering Servant: "Who would have believed our report? And to whom hath the arm of the Lord been revealed? For he shot up right forth as a sapling, and as a root out of a dry ground; he had no form nor comeliness, that we should look upon him, nor beauty that we should delight in him" (Isaiah 53:1,2).

In what sense was the ground in which Jesus grew up "dry ground"? If we look at those things which Israel did not have during the Second Commonwealth and make comparison with what Israel possessed previously, we can acknowledge that Jesus appeared during a "drier" period of Jewish history.

The priests no longer had the *Urim* and *Thummin*, through which for many centuries Israel had obtained the Lord's direct guidance. Also missing from the Second Temple was the Ark of the Covenant, the very symbol of the *shekinah* (the glorious presence of God with His people).

Also conspicuously absent was an heir to the throne of David! There was no semblance of a Kingdom of Israel. Not only was the glory of the former kingdom gone, but what did exist — Judea, Samaria, Galilee, Decapolis, and so forth — was subject to Imperial Rome, and the Jewish people were suppressed in their own homeland.

Without the full light of God's guidance, the glory of His presence, and the favor of national freedom, the soil of the Second Commonwealth clearly was "dry," compared with its former blessing.

We can see how great the dearth was when we examine the responses to Jesus' healings. The people glorified God and said, "We never have seen anything like this!" (Mark 2:12). Yet we do read of wonderful healings in the Old Testament under such people as Abraham (Genesis 20:17), Moses (Numbers 12), Elisha (2 Kings 4:32-37; 5:10); Isaiah (Isaiah 38:1-22), and so forth.

David affirmed that the Lord does heal all our diseases (Psalm 103:3). Healing was known in the Old Testament, but later it became quite scarce. When Jesus came healing by the power of God, multitudes thronged Him, because there was nowhere else to go except to the Pool of Siloam in Jerusalem.

The saddest dearth of all was in the failure of the established religious leadership to recognize the impoverishment of the nation and to look to Him who is "the Restorer of

Israel, and Light to the Gentiles" (Isaiah 49:6); that is, Jesus the promised Messiah!

Consider some of the problems that had developed with the scribes and teachers. In former times, teachers and scribes, such as Ezra, "...read in the book in the law distinctly, and gave the sense, and caused them to understand the reading" (Nehemiah 8:8). This was done for the benefit of the common person.

Yet in Jesus' day, many scribes and teachers made the duties of the scripture grievous and difficult, and Jesus openly denounced such abuses (Matthew 23:1-4). The Bible relates that "the common people heard him gladly" (Mark 12:37).

Why did the common people flock to Him? It is because He offered healing, compassion, and a clear, simple teaching about God that all, even children, could understand. They sought Jesus simply because their needs were not being met in the dry ground of that period of time.

An example is furnished through the Law concerning the offering to be made when a leper is healed (Leviticus 14:1-32). God gave this commandment, knowing that lepers would be healed from time to time. Healing was part of the Covenant (Exodus 23:25); therefore, healing belonged to Israel. When Jesus healed a certain leper in Matthew 8:3,4, He told the man to go to the priest and take the offering that Moses commanded for such cases in Leviticus! The priest knew his duties concerning this rite from his schooling in the Torah, but we wonder how long it had been since a leper had been healed in Israel, and someone had occasion to make this offering.

Certainly Jesus carried within Himself a river of life which was not diminished by the conditions of the day.

As the camel was known as the bearer of man's physical burdens in old days, much more is Jesus the Bearer of Burdens for the whole world! In Isaiah 53, we find that the Suffering Messiah carries our sins, illnesses, sorrows, and griefs.

Quoting from the Jewish Publication Society's translation of Isaiah 53:4,5, we find these words: "Surely our diseases he did bear, and our pains he carried; whereas we did esteem him stricken, smitten of God and afflicted. But he was wounded because of our transgressions, he was crushed because of our iniquities: the chastisement of our welfare was upon him, and with his stripes we were healed."

Sin is the biggest burden of all! Jesus died for the sins of Israel and for the sins of the whole world (John 11:50-52). Sickness is also a terrible human burden.

Jesus was beaten with a Roman whip in order that we might be healed. Sorrow and grief was another terrible burden that He carried as He experienced the rejection of those for whom He cared so deeply.

By simply reading Isaiah 53, the description of God's Suffering Servant, we gain a tremendous insight into the love of our Creator for His creation. It fell upon Jesus' shoulders to bear the burden of all that oppressed humanity. In Him was fulfilled the scripture which says, "The reproaches of them that reproached You, Lord, fell on me" (Psalm 69:9).

When we see *gimel*, we are immediately reminded of the greatest Burden Bearer of history — Jesus, God's Suffering Servant!

(Pronounced DAH-LET)

Chapter 4
Daleth: The Door

Technical Data: 219 words in the Hebrew Bible begin with *daleth.* Of these, 52 are proper names and places, and 167 are regular words. The Greek equivalent of *daleth* is *delta.* Our English letter is "d."

Jewish Definitions: Jewish writers consulted define *daleth* as "an open doorway." More than the door itself, the idea is implied of "an entrance way or an exit."

Christian Definitions: All lexicons and Bible dictionaries consulted concur on the word "door." John Montgomerie, in his book *The Alphabet of God,* says *daleth* also includes the fact of "entrance, outlet, and escape." James Strong adds, "Something swinging like the valve of a door or a two-leaved gate." *Daleth* can be succinctly defined as "an opening."

Devotional Comments

The fourth letter, *daleth,* comes from the word *deleth,* a door. Of the seven Hebrew words for "door" in the Bible, *deleth* is the one with emphasis on swinging (as a gate) or dangling; it can even mean the door valve itself.

Several scriptures in which the Hebrew word for "door" is *deleth* clearly show that it is the type of door which *opens* and *shuts*. Now let us consider the following five scriptures which use the word *deleth*.

Proverbs 26:14 speaks of a door turning upon its hinges. The first occurrence of *deleth* in the Bible is in Genesis 19:6, where Lot shut the door of his house in order to protect his guests who were inside.

We also read David's prayer in Psalm 141:3, "Set a watch, O Lord, before my mouth; keep the door of my lips." As we know, this is one "door" that can be opened or closed. (It does seem, though, that it is open most of the time!)

Elisha's servant hastily told Jehu that he would be Israel's next king, and then he opened the door and fled (2 Kings 9:1-3,10).

The last example is where Elisha raised a little boy from the dead. Elisha went into the room where the boy was lying, shut the door behind him, and began praying. The boy revived, and his mother came into the room and gratefully found her son alive (2 Kings 4:30-37).

We can equate this type of door with the gate of a city. The gate is open during the daytime in order for the people to go *out* and work in the fields and do whatever business daylight requires. As the gate is open until evening, the people come back *in* through this gate. Then, as night falls, the gate is closed so hostile armies and other enemies are shut out, and the peaceful citizens are safely shut in.

We read in the scriptures that in the Messianic Age the gates of Jerusalem shall not be shut day nor night. They shall be open continually to receive the tribute of all the nations that will come up to Jerusalem in order to honor Israel and submit to her Messiah (Isaiah 60:11).

With King Jesus reigning, Israel will have no fear and no need to shut up the gates at any time. "None shall make them afraid." (See Micah 4:1-4.)

A city with its gates open by day and closed by night is an exact counterpart to a sheepfold with its door. The sheep go out from their fold through the door and munch their way through the pasture all day long. Then, in the evening, they return to the fold, the door is shut, and they safely sleep through the night without fear of wolves or other attackers.

With this in mind, Jesus announced that He *is* the Door. "Truly, truly, I say unto you, I am the door; whoever enters through me will be saved...He will come in, and go out, and find pasture" (John 10:7,9). Through Him we enter into the fold of safety, and through Him we go out to the fields of nourishment.

There is a further revelation concerning Jesus as the Door in the design of the tabernacle which God revealed to Moses. The tabernacle was comprised of the outer court, the holy place, and the holy of holies. The Lord Jesus is the Entrance to each of these parts of the tabernacle, as the following facts will illustrate.

He said, "I am the way, the truth, and the life" (John 14:6). The *way* is the entrance into the outer court; the *truth* is the entrance into the holy place; and the *life* is the entrance into the holy of holies!

The parallel is astounding when we consider the means through which entrance was made available into the outer court, the holy place, and the holy of holies. The worshippers came to the outer court with their animals ready to be sacrificed.

The blood of the animals provided their way to approach God. This we relate to receiving Jesus as Savior, as He is the Lamb of God who takes away the sins of the world!

Next, the priests entered the holy place by first washing at the water laver, which was stationed right outside the door of the tabernacle. This we relate to *baptism*, which purifies our conscience.

Finally, the high priest was able to enter the holy of holies once a year, relying on the light of the *menorah* ("lampstand," or in the English versions "candlestick"), which was in the holy place. The *menorah* was the only source of light inside the tabernacle. This we relate to the Holy Spirit of God, whom Jesus sent, and who illuminates the Word of God to us.

It is more astonishing still when we examine Peter's message to the inhabitants of Jerusalem on the Day of Pentecost. On that occasion (Acts 2:38), Peter proclaimed the three keys to the Kingdom of God:

1. *Repent.* Accept Jesus as God's sacrifice with which you may have access to the outer court. Jesus is the *way*.

2. *Be baptized in the Name of Jesus for the remission of sins.* Come to God's water laver and be rinsed clean, which will prepare you, like the priests of old, to enter into the holy place of the tabernacle. Jesus is the *truth*.

3. *Receive the gift of the Holy Spirit.* By the light that God's Holy Spirit sheds on the Word of God you may see clearly enough to come into the very holy of holies, where only the high priest met with the Lord God once a year. Truly knowing God is everlasting life (John 17:3). Jesus is the *life*.

Peter was announcing more than we may realize. Jesus is the Door into the outer court, the Door into the holy place, and the Door into the holy of holies!

The entire nation of Israel was being invited to come into the innermost presence of God, a privilege which previously was offered only to the high priest!

It is good news that this Door is still open for Israel and also for all people everywhere who will respond to the Lord's invitation.

Daleth is Jesus, the true Door for God's people!

(Pronounced HEY)

Chapter 5
He: Ventilation and Lattice/ Breathing Room

Technical Data: In the Hebrew Bible there are 164 words beginning with *he.* Of these, 44 are proper names and places, and 120 are regular words. The Greek equivalent to *he* is *epsilon.* Our English letter is "h."

Jewish Definitions: The difference between *he* and *heth* is that *he* has an opening between the left vertical line and the horizontal line at the top. This opening to some Jewish writers is a reminder for man to know there is an opening to God for any man who will repent. It shows that God is always ready to accept a penitent person whenever that person is ready to return to Him!

Christian Definitions: James Hastings defines *he* as "a window." Gesenius calls it "a lattice." John MacMillan describes *he* as "an outlook," and adds in a devotional way, "That outlook is Christ." John Montgomerie clarifies *he* as "a criss-crossed window." *Davies-Mitchell Lexicon* defines *he* as "a vent-hole" or "to breathe."

21

Devotional Comments

The fifth Hebrew letter, *he*, represents a window or lattice. In biblical times, windows were either a simple opening in the wall of a building, or the kind of opening in which narrow flat laths of wood were placed in a crisscross manner. The latter type afforded a view of the outside without exposing the inside of the house to public view.

So the two-fold function of the window is to let light inside and to provide a view outside. Certainly this was the case with the first window that is mentioned in the Bible, in Genesis 6:16.

God instructed Noah to build a window in the ark. The ark was equipped with a door so its passengers could enter and exit, but with the door closed, only the window furnished light for those inside and provided a view of conditions on the outside.

There are more than forty-five references to windows and lattices in the Old Testament. Some of them involve familiar stories, such as the account of David's escape from King Saul. David's wife, Michal, was King Saul's daughter. While Saul's soldiers were watching for David to escape, Michal slipped her husband out a window, and David fled undetected (1 Samuel 19:12).

Another well-known passage involving windows is in Daniel 6:10. When Daniel's enemies manipulated King Darius into passing a law forbidding prayer, Daniel did not cease praying. In fact, he made no attempt to even *appear* to submit to this legislation. He continued to pray as always, and he even kept his windows open toward Jerusalem! Therefore, his enemies could plainly observe and hear him in prayer.

Another oft-quoted scripture concerns the beloved bridegroom, who reveals himself to the bride through the lattice: "My beloved stands behind our wall, he looks forth at the windows, showing himself through the lattice" (Song of Songs 2:9 KJV paraphrased).

22

Through the centuries, Jewish and Christian interpreters of the Song of Solomon have seen this story as an allegory of the love between the Lord and His people.

In Volume XI of the scholarly *Jewish Encyclopedia* we find the following: "The oldest known interpretation of the Song is allegorical: the *Midrash* and the *Targum* represent it as depicting the relations between God and Israel. The allegorical conception of it passed over into the Christian Church, and has been elaborated by a long line of writers from Origen down to the present time, the deeper meaning being assumed to be the relation between God or Jesus and the church or the individual soul."

It is also notable that in the *Midrash Zuta*, one of the commentaries on the Song of Songs, there are Messianic interpretations of chapter five, verses two and six.

These verses speak of the beloved one who knocks at the door of the sleeping bride and tries to awaken her. When she finally gets up to open the door, he has withdrawn himself and is gone. The bride is unable to find him at that time, although she runs through the streets looking for him.

So in this romantic story we see an illustration of Jesus revealing Himself to the Bride through her window and patiently knocking at her door.

As light shining through a window illuminates a room, so the Lord God shines through Jesus into our hearts. "God, who commanded the light to shine out of darkness has shined in our hearts, to give the light of the knowledge of God's glory in the face of Jesus the Messiah" (2 Corinthians 4:6 KJV paraphrased).

As a window provides a person with a view of the vastness outside, so through Jesus we have an opening to view the glories of God's kingdom!

Every person has a personal outlook about the world. Looking with the insight that is provided by God's Anointed One, we have a much broader view than we could ever have by relying on our own frame of reference.

Through Jesus, we catch a glimpse of the ages. Through Him we understand the eternal purposes of God for the world and for the complete Redemption of humanity. How much more noble is His all-encompassing view than our limited outlook!

A beautiful scripture that expresses the way that light comes in is Psalm 119:130 *(New King James Version):* "The entrance of Your words gives light." Jesus is God's living Word, and when He enters, it produces a wonderful effect on one's life.

Thinking of the Hebrew letter *he* causes us to think of Jesus, the open window through whom God's light and glory shine to us!

(Pronounced VAHV)

Chapter 6
Vav: Hook or Nail

Technical Data: Hebrew words starting with *vav* are very few. There are only 10 of these words, seven being proper names and places. Three are regular words and include the word *vav* itself.

Originally the letter *vav* was the counterpart of the Greek *digamma*, the sixth letter of the early Greek alphabet. Later scholars compare *vav* with the Greek letter *upsilon*. The Greek *digamma* dropped out of the alphabet in the passage of time. The Latins converted the *digamma* and made it the letter "f." Our English letter is "v" or "w."

Jewish Definitions: One Jewish author consulted stayed with the "hook" definition. He referred to the courtyard of the tabernacle *(mishkan)* surrounded by curtains suspended from hooks placed at the top of pillars.

The scriptural name for these hooks is *vavel ha'amudim.* The word "hook" *(vav)* does appear thirteen times in Exodus, describing a part of the tabernacle in the wilderness.

Christian Definitions: Gesenius defines *vav* as "a connector" — nail or hook. Hastings says, "Nail-peg or a hook for hanging things on." John Montgomerie sees it as a fulfillment of Isaiah 22:23 and refers to the Messiah as "a nail in a sure place." John MacMillan defines *vav* as "a nail-hook or a means of fixing two different things."

Devotional Comments

This sixth letter of the Hebrew alphabet is quite remarkable. *Vav* is a nail which is fastened to the wall inside a house, thus serving as a hook from which objects may be hung. (See Ezekiel 15:3; Isaiah 22:25.) The nail not only could be a hook on a wall, but also a hook to support a curtain (Exodus 38:10-12).

As was mentioned in the word study, the Hebrew words *vavel ha'amudim* in Exodus 38 means "hooks of the pillars" or "nails of the pillars."

There is a curious phenomenon regarding the letter *vav*. The single letter *vav* is the word "and" in Hebrew. The word "and" is used excessively in Hebrew and Aramaic, functioning in a way that is not typical of other languages.

For example, in a historical narrative "and" may begin every sentence of a paragraph, as in First Samuel 30:17-21 (KJV paraphrased):

"And David smote them...and none escaped...And David recovered all that the Amalekites had carried away; and David rescued his two wives. And there was nothing lacking to them...And David took all the flocks and the herds...And David came to the two hundred men...and they went forth to meet David, and to meet the people that were with him; and when David came near to the people, he saluted them."

An English teacher would flunk a student for writing a paragraph like that, but in Hebrew it is perfectly appropriate. "And" is a conjunction which is a part of speech that joins two ideas or two parts of a sentence or a phrase. In Hebrew, it is as if the two ideas are "nailed" together with the letter *vav* (the hook).

In Ezra 9:8 we have a unique verse that refers to a nail. Ezra, in the midst of confessing all the sins of the nation of

Israel, broke out into thanksgiving for the good things God had done for the remnant.

Ezra remarks, "the Lord God has shown us grace; he has left us a remnant to escape, and to give us a nail in His holy place." It was the returning *remnant* that gave Israel a nail (a sure, steadfast hook to firmly hang onto) in God's holy place — Jerusalem.

The most wonderful biblical reference to a nail is found in Isaiah 22:20-25. In reading this passage and the five verses leading up to it, we learn that a man named Shebna, who was the king's steward, was going to be demoted from his position and carried into captivity, even though he had been as secure as a nail in a wall. (We read of Shebna's impending downfall in verses 15-19 and 25.)

The Lord speaks through Isaiah that Eliakim (whose name means "who God raises up" and who was God's choice for Shebna's office) will govern in Shebna's stead and even be clothed in his regal garments.

Furthermore, God says that He will lay the key of the house of David upon Eliakim's shoulder so that when Eliakim opens it, no one can shut it; and when he shuts it, no one can open it. Then the Lord says, "And I will fasten him as a nail in a sure place, and he shall be for a glorious throne to his father's house" (verse 23).

Finally the Lord says that they shall hang upon him all the glory of his father's house, from small to large items. We know that this prophecy refers to the life of Eliakim, the son of Hilkiah, who was later promoted to the position Isaiah described.

In Isaiah 36 and 37 we see that in an hour of national crisis, it was Eliakim who faced the Assyrian emissaries outside Jerusalem's walls. Furthermore, it was Eliakim who delivered urgent messages between King Hezekiah and the prophet Isaiah.

Since we know that both Hezekiah and Isaiah were direct descendants of David, the key of the house of David was certainly "laid upon Eliakim's shoulder." Isaiah 37:2 says that Eliakim was over the royal household. Nevertheless, the prophecy concerning Eliakim has a much greater fulfillment.

The greater Son, upon whom all the glory of His Father's house is to rest, is the Lord Jesus our Messiah. Jesus Himself quoted the words of Isaiah's prophecy and applied it to Himself, declaring that He *has* the key of David. He opens and no one can shut; He shuts and no one can open (Revelation 3:7).

And it is Jesus infinitely more than Eliakim who is fastened as a nail in a sure place in order to be for a glorious throne to His Father's house. His genealogical father was David (Matthew 1:1; Luke 1:27; Mark 10:47), and sitting upon the throne of David, He will be the glory of David's house and of all Israel (Isaiah 9:7; Luke 2:32; Daniel 7:13,14).

Zechariah prophesied that "the house of David shall be like *God*, like the Angel of the Lord" (Zechariah 12:8 *NKJV*). This verse gives us a glimpse of the Son of David's divinity and glory and of the glory of His redeemed brethren, the sons of Jacob.

Jesus' own Father, out of whom He came, is the Lord God Almighty, and certainly Jesus as the Heir of God's kingdom will be the ultimate glory of God's house. And, finally, it is Jesus who is the genuine "root and offspring of David" (Revelation 22:16). Certainly, He is the Nail in a Sure Place, holding up the glory of the Father's house.

When we see the letter *vav*, we see Jesus, who is strong and noble enough to bear all the glory of the kingdom, and who joins us to God and to one another!

(Pronounced ZAH-YIN)

Chapter 7

Zayin: The Sword of the Lord

Technical Data: The seventh letter of the Hebrew alphabet is *zayin*, which means "a weapon." Its very shape is reminiscent of a dagger or a sword. Words beginning with the letter *zayin* total 192. Of these, 50 are proper names and places, and 142 are regular words. The comparative Greek letter is *zeta*, and our English letter is "z."

Jewish Definitions: One Jewish writer consulted says of *zayin*, "The letter is shaped like a spear, indicating that man's sustenance is obtained by his struggle. The word for bread *(lechem)* is cognate with the word for war *(lacham)*. The struggle for daily bread in early history caused man to struggle against his fellow man for his existence."

Christian Definitions: All the lexicons and Bible dictionaries consulted were unanimous on *zayin* meaning "a weapon." The Hebrew Bible does have references to "the sword of the Lord." This has Messianic overtones.

29

Devotional Comments

The seventh letter, *zayin*, means "weapon" or "sword." Its shape is clearly similar to that of a sword. In our day of advanced weaponry, we tend to miss many applications of truth, and we perhaps unconsciously dismiss the sword as being primitive or dated.

Actually, the sword was tremendously effective in the following five ways: (1) as a means of attacking the enemy; (2) as a means of protecting the defenseless; (3) as a means of deterring crime; (4) as a means of avenging the deaths of innocent people; and (5) as a means of judgment against nations which transgressed against God.

Let us examine scriptural examples of each of these, beginning with *the sword of attack.* In Joshua we read that God commanded Israel to destroy all the Canaanites. In Joshua 10:28-40, we read of six cities — Makkedah, Libnah, Lachish, Eglon, Hebron, and Debir — which Joshua wiped out.

Six times in this passage we read that Joshua and the Israelites *smote each city with the edge of the sword.* In the life of David, we also have several such attacks against the Philistines.

Next we see the sword as *a means to protect and rescue the defenseless.* In Esther 9:5, we find that Haman's plan for the annihilation of all the Jews was overturned, and the king gave the Jews the right to destroy those who had planned their destruction: "Then the Jews smote all their enemies with the stroke of the sword...."

Concerning the sword as *a deterrent to crime,* we read in Romans 13:3,4 *(The Amplified Bible):*

> **For civil authorities are not a terror to [people of] good conduct, but to [those of] bad behavior. Would you have no dread of him who is in authority? Then do what is right and you will receive his approval and commendation.**

> **For he is God's servant for your good. But if you do wrong, [you should dread him and] be afraid, for he does not bear and wear the sword for nothing. He is God's servant to execute His wrath (His punishment, His vengeance) on the wrongdoer.**

A good example of this is found in Numbers 25:1-15. Phinehas, the grandson of Aaron the high priest, took a javelin and speared an Israelite man and a Midianite woman who were bringing a type of fornication worship into the camp of Israel. What they were doing caused the death of 24,000 Israelites in one day!

What Phinehas did with his javelin not only turned God's anger away from Israel, but it was a tremendous deterrent to such behavior in the future! Anyone thinking of joining up with Midianite idolatries was bound to reconsider.

The sword *avenged the murder of innocent people,* as in First Samuel 15:33, where Samuel killed wicked Agag, king of the Amalekites. As he was about to slay Agag, Samuel said to him, "As your sword has made women *childless,* so shall your mother be childless among women" *(NKJV).* This is a fitting verdict for the murderer of innocent children.

Now let us consider how the sword is frequently spoken of as *a means of national judgment.* Ezekiel particularly speaks of the sword, and so do Isaiah and Jeremiah. (See Ezekiel chapters 5, 6, and 33; Jeremiah 14:15-18; Isaiah 65:12.)

Jesus accurately predicted the fall of Jerusalem, the destruction of the Temple, and the scattering of the Jewish people (Luke 21:20-24; Matthew 23:38-24:2). Jesus' exact words concerning the people of Judea were, "They will fall by the edge of the sword, and be led away captive into all nations" (Luke 21:24 *NKJV*).

Jesus also spoke of Israel's regathering and Redemption, as did Ezekiel and Jeremiah, both of whom speak of the Jewish nation as "regathered from the sword" or "the survivors of the sword" (Jeremiah 31:2; Ezekiel 38:8).

We have just considered five uses for the sword. Now we will take a look at a few scriptures which link the Messiah to a mighty weapon of the Lord. In Isaiah 49:1-13, we find someone saying:

"The Lord has called me from the womb; from inside my mother has he made mention of my name. He has made

31

his mouth like a sharp sword; in the shadow of his hand he has hidden me, and made me a polished shaft; in his quiver he has hidden me, and said unto me, You are my servant, O Israel, in whom I will be glorified."

As this portion goes on to describe the accomplishments of the servant, it becomes clear that it is speaking of someone more specific and individual than the nation Israel.

This servant was formed from the womb to bring Jacob again to the Lord, to gather Israel (so it cannot be that the nation of Israel was formed from the womb to restore and gather itself), to raise up the tribes of Jacob, and to restore the preserved of Israel.

In addition, this passage of scripture says that the servant in question will be glorious in the eyes of the Lord *even while Israel is not yet gathered;* he will be a light to the Gentiles, and he will be God's salvation unto the end of the Earth.

There is only one Person in history who could possibly fulfill these requirements, and that is Jesus of Nazareth! He is the One whose mouth is like a sharp sword, as it is said in Isaiah 49:2 and again in Revelation 19:15, referring to the return of Jesus to rule all nations: "And out of His mouth goes a sharp sword, that with it he should smite the nations; and he shall rule them with a rod of iron...."

How similar this is to Isaiah's description of the Messiah as a descendant of David upon whom the Spirit of God would rest (Isaiah 11:1-4):

> And there shall come forth a rod out of the stem of Jesse, and a Branch shall grow out of his roots:
>
> And the spirit of the Lord shall rest upon him, the spirit of wisdom and understanding, the spirit of counsel and might, the spirit of knowledge and of the fear of the Lord;
>
> And shall make him of quick understanding in the fear of the Lord: and he shall not judge after the sight of his eyes, neither reprove after the hearing of his ears:
>
> But with righteousness shall he judge the poor, and reprove with equity for the meek of the earth: and he shall

smite the earth: with the rod of his mouth, and with the breath of his lips shall he slay the wicked.

In the Book of Hebrews we read, "The Word of God is quick [alive], and powerful, and sharper than any two-edged sword, piercing even to the dividing asunder of soul and spirit, and of the joints and marrow, and is a discerner of the thoughts and intents of the heart" (Hebrews 4:12).

God's Word has a way of slicing to the heart of a matter and exposing what is truly inside us. This is how it was when Jesus spoke: The thoughts of people's hearts were exposed!

It is astonishing to read Jesus' answers to situations which confronted Him — answers so compassionate and righteous that seemingly no one could object, yet answers that often provoked cries of outrage. What could possibly account for this but the penetrating and revealing nature of His words?

Jesus is frequently called "the Word" in the New Testament. (See John 1:1,14; 1 John 1:1,2; Revelation 19:13.) We understand also that the Word of God is the spiritual sword (Ephesians 6:17).

So the biblical references to a sword coming from Messiah's mouth to strike the nations clearly refer to His *word*, which He will set forth as Earth's true and righteous King in the Messianic Age, which is approaching.

His word will be God's word, the *final* word on all human affairs. Thus shall Zion's once-rejected King rule valiantly and victoriously in all places of God's dominion.

In that day, Jesus, the Prince of Peace, will totally abolish warfare, and "nation shall not lift up sword against nation, neither shall they learn war anymore" (Isaiah 2:4 *NKJV*).

Why will warfare be gone forever? It is because the only defense, protection, and vindication we will ever need will be provided by our Messiah, whose mouth God fashioned like a sharp sword. Long live King Jesus!

When we see *zayin*, we think of the sharp sword coming out of Jesus' mouth — the sword with which He will subdue all nations for God's kingdom!

(Pronounced KHET)

Chapter 8
Cheth: A Fenced-in or Enclosed Area

Technical Data: The eighth letter of the Hebrew alphabet is *cheth.* Note: We, along with most sources, have chosen to spell this letter *cheth.* However, several modern lexical sources, among them *The New King James Version, The New International Version, The New American Bible,* and *The New American Standard Bible,* spell it *heth.* Words in the Hebrew Bible starting with *cheth* number 625. Of these, 182 are proper names and places, and 438 are regular words.

The Greek equivalent to *cheth* is *eta.* In English, we would use the letter "kh" or "ch" to represent the sound of *cheth.* This sound does not exist in the English language. It may be compared to the "ch" in the Scottish word *loch.*

Jewish Definitions: One Jewish writer stated, "The shape of the letter *cheth* alludes to sin. The top of the *cheth* as it is written in the Torah scrolls is not straight, but has a wavering line that rises and falls. This alludes to the inconsistent spirit of a sinner."

Christian Definitions: Interpreter's Dictionary defines *cheth* as "a hedge or a fence." *Davies-Mitchell Lexicon* says of *cheth*, "to enclose." *Hastings' Dictionary* uses the word "palisade," and John MacMillan describes *cheth* as "a fence or protection from danger."

Devotional Comments

The eighth letter, *cheth*, signifies "a fence." Take a moment to see how similar in appearance this letter is to the letter *he*, the fifth letter.

You can see that in the case of the letter *he* (the window) there is a little opening between the top of the left stem and the top bar of the letter, whereas in the case of the letter *cheth*, the gap is closed.

So it is with a fence, which encloses and surrounds the property that it is designed to protect. A fence is usually constructed for one of two reasons.

First is the need to protect the property inside. (A fence not only protects what is inside, but also serves as a barrier for those outside.) Second is the need to visibly define property boundaries in order that everyone may know where an individual's property begins and ends. As we look at this subject in the Bible, both of these concepts will become apparent.

In the English language we find that "fence" essentially means "defense." In *Webster's Seventh New Collegiate Dictionary* under "fence" we find the first meaning to be "a means of protection: defense"; and the second meaning to be "a barrier intended to prevent escape or intrusion or to mark a boundary."

The word itself comes from the Middle English "fens," which is short for "defens" (defense). There is no shortage of scriptural assurances that the Lord Himself is the Defense of His people!

David affirms, "God is my defense" (Psalm 59:9,16). Also, in the Psalms we find these words: "My defense is of God, who saves the upright in heart" (Psalm 7:10 *NKJV*).

"The Lord is my defence; and my God is the rock of my refuge" (Psalm 94:22). "The Lord is our defence; and the Holy One of Israel is our king" (Psalm 89:18).

All these verses clearly tell of the Lord's ownership, protection, and preservation of His redeemed ones. He speaks in a very possessive way of Israel:

> **But now thus saith the Lord that created thee, O Jacob, and he that formed thee, O Israel, Fear not: for I have redeemed thee, I have called thee by thy name; thou art *mine*.**
>
> **Isaiah 43:1**

Throughout scripture we also read of God's particular jealousy over Jerusalem. For example, "Thus says the Lord of hosts; I am jealous for Jerusalem and for Zion with a great jealousy" (Zechariah 1:14). This possessive determinism on the part of God leads Him to defend Jerusalem in a spectacular way.

Zechariah 2:5 states, "For I, saith the Lord, will be unto her [Jerusalem] a wall of fire round about, and will be the glory in the midst of her." Most expressive is Isaiah 31:5: "As birds flying, so will the Lord of hosts defend Jerusalem; defending also he will deliver it; and passing over he will preserve it."

Also, in Second Kings 19:34 we see God's promise through the prophet Isaiah to spare Jerusalem: "For I will defend this city, to save it, for mine own sake, and for my servant David's sake." These scriptures suggest a fence or a hedge of protection around God's people.

In Isaiah 5:1-7, we have a touching account of the Lord's relationship to Israel. God calls Israel His vineyard. He dug out the stones, planted the choicest vines in "a very fruitful hill," placed a fence around it, built a tower and a winepress in it, and then came looking for His harvest — righteous people.

Not finding a satisfactory harvest, He resolved to break down the hedge along with its wall and allow it to be trampled and neglected.

The word "hedge" in verse 5 is the noun *mesukah* in Hebrew, which is built from the verb *suwk*, meaning "to shut in for protection or restraint; to fence up, to make a hedge."

So Isaiah speaks at different times both of God's hedging Jerusalem in with His protection and of His withdrawing His protection in times of national distress as a result of sin.

He concludes with this final verse of his song: "For the vineyard of the Lord of hosts is the house of Israel, and the men of Judah his pleasant plant: and he looked for judgment, but behold oppression; for righteousness, but behold a cry" (verse 7).

The two most significant occasions of God's withdrawal of His protection from Jerusalem were, of course, the destruction of the First Temple by the Babylonians and the destruction of the Second Temple by the Romans.

Each occasion was clearly preceded by God's warnings through His prophets that Jerusalem would be taken, the Temple would be destroyed, and the Jewish people would go into exile. In both cases, the warnings were not believed by the majority of God's people.

Jeremiah accurately prophesied the first catastrophe (Jeremiah 7:1-15; 25:7-12; 26:1-24), and Jesus was the *only* prophet of His day to accurately predict the disaster which befell Jerusalem in the year A.D. 70. (See Luke 19:41-44; 21:5-24; Matthew 24:1,2.)

Consider Jerusalem, unique among the world's cities in tragedy and in destiny. God says that someday Jerusalem shall be called "the throne of the Lord" (Jeremiah 3:17); and Jesus called it "the city of the great King" (Matthew 5:35). The future glory of Jerusalem far exceeds both the glory and the suffering of its past.

When shall we see the prophecies fulfilled concerning Jerusalem's unending peace flowing like a river? When will "violence and destruction be no longer heard in the land"? It is when Israel is restored to full favor with God and is protected by the wonderful embrace of Messiah Jesus, the Prince of

Peace. At that time, the fence of protection around His people will be the Lord Himself!

At the present time, even in Jerusalem, the city of the great King, one may be exposed to life-threatening dangers. But in the protective hedge of the Messiah's care, we find a place where "no disaster shall befall you, nor any plague come near your dwelling" (Psalm 91:10).

To whom does this promise of safety belong? The answer is found in the preceding verse: to those who have made the Lord Most High their *refuge* and *habitation*.

If anyone wishes to know what it is like to know God's care, defense, and warm protection as revealed in His Messiah, it can be discovered in this description of the great Redeemer in Isaiah 40:11:

> **He shall feed his flock like a shepherd: he shall gather the lambs with his arm, and carry them in his bosom, and shall gently lead those that are with young.**

Jesus is the Defense, the Enclosure, the Protective Hedge that enables us to face life's dangers, injustices, and uncertainties without fear. When we see *cheth,* we think of Him who is our great Protector!

(Pronounced TET)

Chapter 9
Teth: The Serpent

*T*echnical Data: *Teth* is the ninth letter of the Hebrew alphabet. There are 100 words in the Hebrew Bible starting with the letter *teth*. Of these, 15 are proper names, and 85 are regular words. The Greek equivalent is *theta.* Our English letter is "t." Originally, *teth* was drawn in such a way that it looked like a coiled snake; hence, the serpent definition.

Jewish Definitions: The *Midrash* defines *teth* as "alluding to the Hebrew word for mud *(tiyt).* This is symbolic of physical matter from which man's body was created and to which he will return."

Christian Definitions: Hastings' *Dictionary* defines *teth* as "curvature or coiled snake." Gesenius states, "besides serpent, it is something rolled or twisted together." *International Standard Bible Encyclopedia* departs from the snake category and defines *teth* as "a package or a cake or bread."

John MacMillan states, "*teth* is a serpent." He says that *teth* is most suggestive of "energy, subtlety, venomous, and deadly." He further comments, "Evil has all these elements. *Teth* reminds us that Messiah shall overcome all evil."

41

Devotional Comments

The ninth letter, *teth*, represents a serpent, which the shape of the letter closely resembles. More than anything else in creation, the serpent evokes universal disgust and repulsion. Nevertheless, the serpent originally was a graceful, gliding creature, which is not what we picture serpents to be today. As a matter of fact, the Hebrew word *seraph*, which means a graceful angelic being in a fiery form, is sometimes translated "serpent" or "fiery flying serpent" in the Bible!

The splendor of this charming creature became corrupted as a result of sin's entrance into the universe. Thus, the most beautiful of creatures was transformed into the most revolting of creatures, maintaining in its slippery means of navigation only a vestige of its original gracious style and bearing.

It has been remarked that women seemingly have the greatest antagonism to serpents. Perhaps this instinctive antipathy, which Genesis 3:15 calls enmity or hatred, has been part of the genetic and emotional makeup of the human race since Eden.

Not only does the serpent generally incite fear and loathing in people; it also is the very symbol of *sin* and the *curse* throughout scripture. This linking of the serpent to sin and the curse is what we are about to examine.

The first reference to the serpent in the Bible, in Genesis 3, identifies him as the instigator of sin, the tempter, and the deceiver. Later, when the children of Israel complained against Moses in the wilderness, fiery serpents swarmed among them, causing many to die from poisonous bites.

In the New Testament, we read that the serpent in the beginning beguiled the human race through his subtlety (2 Corinthians 11:3). In Revelation, this one who deceived the nations is called "that old serpent, which is the devil, and Satan" (Revelation 20:2). These verses alone show that the serpent is the symbol of evil.

There is something insidious about every aspect of the serpent's furtive behavior. His venom is another proof of his malicious character. Added to this is the serpent's reputation for wisdom, cunning, calculation, a hypnotic gaze, and mes-merizing movements. In total, he is a most undesirable sort of creature!

What does this revolting reptile have to do with our study? After the Israelites had been attacked by poisonous serpents, they asked Moses to pray for the removal of this curse from their camp. The people were urgently in need of forgiveness and healing. They sincerely repented, and God in return instructed Moses to do something that sounds quite strange.

The people came to Moses and said, "We have sinned, for we have spoken against the Lord, and against you; pray unto the Lord, that He take away the serpents from us." And when Moses prayed for the people, the Lord said to him:

> **Make thee a fiery serpent, and set it upon a pole: and it shall come to pass, that every one that is bitten, when he looks upon it, shall live.**

> **And Moses made a serpent of brass, and put it upon a pole, and it came to pass, that if a serpent had bitten any man, when he beheld the serpent of brass, he lived.**

> **Numbers 21:8,9**

Take a moment to consider the implications of this account in Numbers 21. What human being, having been painfully bitten and now swollen with serpent's venom, would even want to *look* at another serpent? If the serpent was considered repulsive under normal circumstances, how much more so when serpents raced through the camp, attack-ing many families and causing fright and distress!

Imagine that you personally had been bitten, and that the only way to escape death was to look up at the serpent on the pole. Would you want to look at it? Certainly God knew that the serpent would be a repulsive sight, offensive to human "sensibilities," but still He *demanded* that they look upon it in order to be healed.

Employing a brass serpent to cure serpent bites may seem to be an irony, yet it is a spiritual illustration of the nature of homeopathic medical science. This type of treatment involves injecting substances which, were they put into healthy persons, would cause sickness. Some vaccines contain a minute amount of the very thing they serve to prevent.

This law of homeopathic treatment is *similia similibus curentur*, which says, "Let likes be treated with likes." And this is where Jesus comes in.

In John 3:14,15, we read these startling words: "...as Moses lifted up the serpent in the wilderness, even so must the Son of man be lifted up, in order that whoever believes in Him should not die, but have eternal life."

This shows us a striking comparison of the brass serpent suspended on the pole and Jesus suspended on the cross. In both cases, Israel was *commanded* to look up and truly behold the one that was lifted up. God said that if they would *look*, they would *live*. Not only was this forgiveness and healing offered to Israel, but also to the whole world.

Jesus said, "When I am lifted up from the earth, I will draw *all men* unto me." He said these words in order to specify what type of death He was going to die (John 12:32,33).

How could He be certain that all men would be drawn to Him? It is because all men have been bitten by the venomous serpent of sin; all have suffered through sickness, which is endemic to humanity; and all will die from sin and sickness unless they look up and see this awe-producing spectacle on the pole.

Many artists have painted imaginative portraits of the death of Jesus, but none can do greater justice to the picture than God Himself, whose words in Isaiah 53 perfectly define the Redeemer's suffering, the horrifying effect His pierced body had on the onlookers, the reluctance of the people even to look at Him, and the nature of His death "for the transgression of *My* people."

Consider this description of the foreordained Savior of Israel and the entire world as it appears in the *Jewish Publication Society's* version of Isaiah 52:14 and 53:2,3:

> His visage was marred unlike that of a man, and his form unlike that of the sons of men....
>
> He had no form nor comeliness that we should *look* upon him, nor beauty that we should desire him.
>
> He was despised and forsaken of men, a man of pains, and acquainted with disease, and as one from whom men hide their face: he was despised, and we esteemed him not.

In other words, the sight was so unbearable that no one wanted to look! Eyes turned away, unable to continue taking in the picture. We did not wish to see it, but still God states, "Look and live!"

The complete spiritual restoration of the nation of Israel will occur when the people look at their sacrificed Messiah and live:

> And I will pour upon the house of David, and upon the inhabitants of Jerusalem, the spirit of grace and of supplications: and they shall *look* upon Me whom they have pierced, and they shall mourn for Him as one mourns for his only son, and shall be in bitterness for Him, as one that is in bitterness for his firstborn.
>
> Zechariah 12:10

Jesus said further, "When you have lifted up the Son of Man, then you shall *know* that I am he" (John 8:28). We will know that He is who? We will know that He is *the one* spoken of in Isaiah 53; in fact, the only One in history whose sacrificial death for sin and whose Atonement for transgressors could possibly fulfill this prophecy.

The third person masculine singular (He, Him, His) appears 39 times in Isaiah 53 in reference to this Righteous Servant. Thirty-nine references in 12 short verses to someone called "he." Jesus was clearly saying that all would be able to recognize Him as the "he" in question in this monumental prophecy.

When Jesus was lifted up on the cross, and the events which Isaiah prophesied began to occur, it would become obvious that Jesus was the sin offering of Isaiah 53.

What do you personally see when you think of the death of Jesus? Is it just the death of someone historical, or can you see in it the extent that God's love could go for a sick and sinful humanity?

The scriptures definitely show that Jesus lived a sinless, righteous, blameless, and holy life. Yet He was "made in the likeness of sinful flesh." He was even willing to be made into an object from which people would instantly recoil — as they had from that serpent on the pole — if only their salvation, healing, and Redemption would be the result! *Such unselfishness and humility has never existed in any other man to the degree that it did in Jesus of Nazareth.*

When we see *teth* the serpent, we think of the despised One lifted high on a pole in order that all nations could look at Him and live!

(Pronounced YODE)

Chapter 10
Yod: Open the Hand of Power

Technical Data: Yod is the smallest letter of the Hebrew alphabet. It is almost as small as our apostrophe mark! Jesus referred to the Hebrew alphabet when He said in Matthew 5:18 that not one jot (*yod*) or tittle (the written apex of a Hebrew letter) shall in any wise pass from the law until all be fulfilled.

The words in the Hebrew Bible beginning with *yod* total 542. Of these, 304 are proper names and places, and 238 are regular words. The Greek equivalent is *iota* (the smallest Greek letter). Our English letter is "i."

Jewish Definitions: Jewish writers consulted interpret the *yod* or hand as denoting power and possession. In Deuteronomy 14:25, the closed hand suggests ownership. In Deuteronomy 15:11, the open hand suggests having the power and generosity to be able to bless others.

Christian Definitions: Most of the writers consulted define *yod* as "hand." In Ethiopic, *yod* is the "right hand," suggestive of power. Strong's defines *yod* as "the open hand indicating power, means, and direction."

John MacMillan goes another direction and describes the hands as having 10 fingers. This, in turn, alludes to 10 words, 10 commandments, or practical Christian living. No matter what spiritual interpretations or allegories the word *yod* contains, the basic meaning is still "hand." Messianic sections of scripture call our attention to "the hand of the Lord."

Devotional Comments

The tenth letter, *yod*, signifies "a hand." The Hebrew word for hand is *yad*, from which comes *yod*. This small letter stands for the number 10 in the Hebrew manner of numbering. It has been mentioned we have 10 fingers on our hands with which we can count the Ten Commandments God gave.

With two hands a person can hold and embrace the Holy Scriptures, which is one of the great privileges of being human. This means we can hold the oracles of God; we can ponder God's thoughts; and we can hide His words in our heart.

Although the hand is a small part of the human body, we would nearly be unable to function in life if our hands were missing. Similarly, the letter *yod* is the smallest letter in the Hebrew alphabet, yet it begins the most important words in the Hebrew language.

Foremost of these, of course, is the Lord's Holy Name, which some researchers have attempted to spell as "Yahweh," and which has been Anglicized into the familiar spelling "Jehovah." Next there is the name of Jesus *(Yeshua)* and the words it comes from: salvation *(yesha)*; Jerusalem *(Yerushalayim)*; Judah *(Yehudah)*; Jew *(Yehudi)*; Jeshurun *(Yeshurun)*, which means "the upright one"; and it is a poetical name for the nation of Israel; Jordan *(Yardan)*; and a seldom-used rabbinic title of the Messiah, *Yinnon*.

According to *Sanhedrin 98b*, *Yinnon* is one of the names of Messiah, based on Psalm 72:17, which some rabbinic authorities read as follows: "Before the sun, Yinnon was his name." This indicates the preexistence of the Messiah. *Yinnon* means "He shall continue," or "He shall flourish."

And He *did* flourish, this root out of a dry ground. Isaiah 53:10 says concerning the Messiah, "the pleasure of the Lord shall prosper *in his hand.*" If we take a moment and consider what was accomplished by *the hands* of the young man who went about His Father's business, we will see a world of kind and righteous deeds.

We recall that Jairus, a synagogue official, had a 12-year-old daughter who became very ill and died. Jesus went into the child's room, *took her by the hand,* and restored her to life (Matthew 9:25).

In Nazareth, *He laid His hands* on a number of sick people and healed them (Mark 6:5). A desperate father pled with Jesus to heal his deaf son, whose entire childhood had been plagued with violent seizures. Jesus delivered the boy from the tormenting spirits which had troubled him. Then *He took the boy by the hand* and presented him safe and sound to his grateful father (Mark 9:17-27).

Another deaf man, who also had a speech impediment, was brought to Jesus for healing. *He put His fingers* in the man's ears, *touched* the man's tongue, and said, "Be opened!" Immediately the man's hearing and speech were restored (Mark 7:32-35).

He put His hands on the eyes of two blind men, and their sight was restored (Matthew 9:28-30). Jesus even *put forth His hand* and *touched* a leper! Immediately the man's leprosy was cured (Matthew 8:3). *With His hands,* Jesus broke the bread and fish in order to feed a hungry crowd of more than 5,000 people (Matthew 14:19-21).

When Peter began to sink in the tempestuous waves, Jesus *reached out His hand,* as He is known to do, and rescued him (Matthew 14:31). When the disciples were frightened by the glory of God and His voice on the mountain, Jesus *touched them* and told them, "Rise up; do not be afraid" (Matthew 17:7).

These are just a few examples of the kindness that was expressed through the powerful and gentle hands of the Messiah. How true is the scripture Acts 10:38! "God anointed Jesus of Nazareth with the Holy Ghost and with power: who went about doing *good*, and healing all that were oppressed of the devil; for God was with Him."

These hands which expressed healing, comfort, rescue, and tenderness also expressed divine correction. The Old Testament said God's house was supposed to be a house of prayer for all people. Finding God's holy Temple polluted with moneychangers and the selling of animals for sacrifice, Jesus fashioned small cords into a whip and drove out the offenders and the offenses.

This event caused great disruption in the status quo. "By what authority do you do these things? Who gave you this authority?" His fellow countrymen asked.

These words closely parallel those of Moses' fellow Israelites: "Who made *you* a judge over *us?*" Have you ever noticed how easy it is to receive kindnesses, comfort, gifts, and compliments from someone, yet how hard it is to receive correction from anyone, even those who have every right to do the correcting?

There seems to be something deeply rooted in human beings which resists correction! When pride aggravates this already existing condition, people have been known to become absolutely unteachable. Nevertheless, Jesus did not shrink from His duty and right to correct His nation, nor did he neglect any opportunity to heal His people. Such hands inspire wonder and respect!

When we see little *yod*, we think of Jesus, *the very hands of God!* In Isaiah 65:2, God said, "I have spread out *my hands* all the day unto a rebellious people."

God spread out His arms in Jesus, in a wide embrace which reveals His benevolent intent for us all — to be safe in His Messiah's hands!

(Pronounced KAWF)

Chapter 11
Kaph: **Palm of the Hand**

Technical Data: Kaph is the eleventh letter of the Hebrew alphabet. Of the 298 words starting with *kaph* in the Hebrew Bible, 78 are proper names and places, and 220 are regular words. The Greek equivalent is *kappa*, and our English letter is "k."

Jewish Definitions: Jewish writers state that *kaph* means "bent." It has a dual symbolism, standing for the palm of the hand serving as a container and, at the same time, as a measure for what it holds. Ibn Ezra states that *kaph* means "result through mental and physical effort." While *yod* stands for the hand indicating power and possession, *kaph* denotes productivity and accomplishment.

Christian Definitions: Christian writers define *kaph* as: (1) "hollow of the hand," (2) "the palm of the hand," and (3) "a wing." Al Novak says *kaph* is "a bent hand." Dr. James Strong defines it as "the hollow hand, paw, or palm" and states that the figurative definition is "power."

David stated in Psalm 139:5 *(NIV)*, "You hem me in — behind and before; you have laid your hand *[kaph]* upon me."

In this case, *kaph* could mean safety, guidance, restraint, protection, and blessing.

Devotional Comments

The eleventh Hebrew letter, *kaph,* can mean both "palm of the hand" and "wing." The word generally used for "palms" of the hands is *kaph,* and the usual word for "wing" is *kanaph.*

As you can see, these two words are similar, and so are their meanings. What a bent hand or arm is to a person, a wing is to a bird. Furthermore, as the largest part of human efficiency involves the hands at work, so the greatest part of a bird's efficiency involves the wings at work.

So taking the twin concepts of palm of the hand and wing, we shall see a number of relevant biblical references which may be applied to characteristics of the Lord.

One of the most beautiful and tender descriptions of God's parental love for His people is found in Deuteronomy 1:31:

In the wilderness you saw how the Lord God carried you as a father carries his son, all along the way that you went, until you reached this place.

Later in Deuteronomy, we read that God carried Israel as an eagle does its offspring:

The Lord's portion is His people; Jacob is His allotted inheritance.

In a desert land He found him, in a barren and howling waste. He shielded him and cared for him; He guarded him as the apple of His eye,

like an eagle spreads its wings to catch them, and carries them on its wings —

so the Lord alone did lead Jacob.

Deuteronomy 32:9-12

Exodus 19:4 closely parallels the above reference. God instructs Moses to say to the children of Israel, "You have seen what I did unto the Egyptians, and how I carried you on eagles' wings, and brought you unto myself."

As we go further through the Bible, we start finding more metaphors about the Lord's "wings." In Ruth 2:12, Boaz puts this wonderful blessing on his future wife, Ruth, saying, "May the Lord recompense your work, and may a full reward be given you from the Lord God of Israel, under whose wings you have come to trust."

Later, Boaz' great-grandson David prayed, "Keep me as the apple of the eye; hide me under the shadow of thy wings" (Psalm 17:8).

Nowhere in scripture is there a more detailed illustration of the protective wings of God than in Psalm 91:4: "He will cover you with His feathers, and under His wings you will find refuge."

The most familiar verse concerning wings is Malachi 4:2, which has long been associated with the Messiah. (In the Hebrew Bible this verse is Malachi 3:20). It states, "Unto you that fear my name shall the Sun of righteousness arise with healing in his wings."

Many people understand this to illustrate the way the morning sun rises with irradiating shoots of light, beams, or rays, branching out in all directions. In other words, this Sun of righteousness rises with healing in its radiant beams.

One of the most interesting set of scriptures *apropos* of wings concerns the *cherubim*. The word *cherubim* is the plural of *cherub* (*keruv, cheruv,* in Hebrew), the covering angel. There are about 30 references to the wings of the *cherubim* in the Bible.

In Exodus 25:18-20,22, we read part of the amazing instructions which God gave to Moses about the construction of the Ark of the Covenant:

And you shall make two cherubim of gold....

...one cherub on the one end, and the other cherub on the other end...

> And the cherubim shall stretch forth their wings on high, covering the mercy seat with their wings, and their faces shall look one to another; toward the mercy seat shall the faces of the cherubim be....

> And there I will meet with you, and I will commune with you from above the mercy seat, from between the two cherubim which are upon the Ark of the Testimony, concerning everything which I will give you in commandment to the children of Israel.

Imagine that! God met with man from between the two golden *cherubim.* The visible place of God's glory on Earth was covered protectively by the wings of these two "covering angels."

Much has been written about the *shekinah,* or glorious presence of God, which was visible on different biblical occasions, such as when Solomon dedicated the Temple in Jerusalem.

Some have felt that the *shekinah* — in the form of a radiant cloud of glory — was what Moses or Aaron could see between the *cherubim,* and that from this cloud of light God communed with them, and therefore with Israel.

> And the cherubim spread out their wings on high, and covered with their wings over the mercy seat, with their faces one to another; towards the mercy seat were the faces of the cherubim.

> **Exodus 37:9**

This verse describes the finished piece of art work — when the Ark was completed. Because this was the way God chose to manifest His presence to Israel, the psalmist Asaph could write: "Give ear, O Shepherd of Israel, thou that leadest Joseph like a flock; thou that dwellest between the cherubim, SHINE FORTH!" (Psalm 80:1; see also Isaiah 37:16.)

Remember this illustration of the covering angels guarding the place of God's presence, for we will soon refer to it again. But first we must examine some usages of the word *kaph,* as in "palm of the hand." The word *kaph* appears over

200 times in the Bible, but we have chosen only six representative references to show some of its usages.

First, we see *protection,* again involving angels, in Psalm 91:11,12: "He shall give his angels charge over you, to keep you in all your ways. They shall bear you up *in their hands* [*kaph*], lest you dash your foot against a stone."

Next, and akin to this thought, we get a sense of *permanent security* in Isaiah 62:3, where Jerusalem is told, "You shall also be a crown of glory *in the hand* of the Lord, and a royal diadem *in the hand* of your God."

Third, we see *innocent hands,* which denote a state of righteousness. Psalm 24:4 tells us that he who has *clean hands* and a pure heart shall stand in God's holy place. (See also Psalm 26:6, where David says, just before approaching God's altar, "I will *wash my hands* in innocency.")

Then we find the *skillful guidance* of a gentle shepherd being expressed through his hands:

He chose David also His servant, and took him from the sheepfolds:

From following the ewes great with young He brought him to feed Jacob His people, and Israel His inheritance.

So he fed them according to the integrity of his heart; and guided them by *the skilfulness of his hands.*

Psalm 78:70-72

Fifth, we see how essential the hands are for praising God: "Let my prayer be set before thee as incense; and *the lifting up of my hands* as the evening sacrifice" (Psalm 141:2).

Last, we see an *everlasting faithfulness* in the hands of the Messiah.

The Lord...will have mercy on His afflicted people.

But Zion said, The Lord has forsaken me, and my Lord has forgotten me.

Can a woman forget her nursing child, that she would not have compassion on the son of her womb? Yes, they could forget, yet will I not forget you.

Behold, I have engraven you *upon the palms of my hands;* your walls are continually before me.

Isaiah 49:13-16 KJV paraphrased

We may wonder how Jerusalem could possibly be engraved on the palms of God's hands. The New Testament unfolds this mystery, as we see the Redeemer sent from heaven who was pierced in His hands for the sake of His dearly loved nation, and this was done *in Jerusalem. It is Jerusalem which is engraved upon God's hands!*

We have just examined scriptures which can portray Messiah's protective hands, innocent hands, skillful hands, praising hands, and pierced hands. We must also consider Messiah's "wings."

As Jesus wept over His beloved Jerusalem, which He alone knew was soon to be destroyed, He gave this most sorrowful lamentation over the city:

O Jerusalem, Jerusalem, city which kills the prophets and stones them that are sent unto you — how often I would have gathered your children together, as a hen gathers her brood under her wings, but you were not willing.

Behold your Temple is left unto you desolate; and truly I tell you, you shall not see me until the time comes when you shall say, "Blessed is he that comes in the name of the Lord."

Luke 13:34,35 KJV paraphrased

How different the past nineteen centuries could have been for Jerusalem had she simply allowed her King to take her people under His wing! And how secure Jerusalem shall be when she sees Him and comes to trust under His wings, knowing Him to be in truth the Messiah sent from God!

A fuller insight into the glories of His person follows our knowing Him as Redeemer, Messiah, and King of Israel. We come to know Him as the Lord of Glory, the same Mighty One whom the *cherubim* of the Ark of the Covenant were covering, each one facing the place where He dwelled.

In closing this chapter, let us see one more verse which illustrates this very truth. In John 20:11-13, one of Jesus' followers named Miriam came to the sepulchre where Jesus had been buried. At first she stood outside, weeping, but then she bent down and looked inside. She saw two angels who asked her why she was weeping. She told them, "It is because they have taken away my Lord..." (verse 13).

She recognized Jesus as her *Lord*, and so did the angels. One angel was positioned "at the head, and the other at the feet, where the body of Jesus had lain" (verse 12). These angels were simply stationed in their accustomed position in covering the Lord of Glory — guarding Him silently, faithful as they had always been to this duty for which they had been created.

Kaph is the Messiah's pierced hands or His enfolding wings under which we shall trust securely forever. *No one is able to take us out of His hand!* (See John 10:28.)

(Pronounced LAH-MED)

Chapter 12

Lamed: Ox-Goad or Staff

Technical Data: Lamed is the twelfth letter of the Hebrew alphabet. Only 156 words in the Hebrew Bible start with *lamed,* 44 of which are proper names and places. The Greek equivalent is *lambda,* and our English letter is "l."

Jewish Definitions: The *Mishnah* (Amos 1:17; 3:12) points out *lamad* (related to *lamed*) as referring both to teaching and to learning. The cattle goad is called "teacher of cattle." All study of God's Word is insufficient if it is not translated into action. Study is not the ultimate goal; rather, the deeds derived from that study.

Christian Definitions: Christian writers define *lamed* as "an ox goad." *Davies-Mitchell Lexicon* calls it "a staff." John MacMillan editorializes by saying, "Shamgar's ox goad (from *lamad)* was an uncouth weapon, but it saved a country" (Judges 3:31). James Strong defines *lamed* as from *lamad,* "to goad; by implication to teach." He further adds that Oriental teachers used a goad or a rod as an incentive for learning.

59

Devotional Comments

The twelfth letter of the Hebrew alphabet, *lamed*, represents an ox goad. The Hebrew word for ox goad is *malmad*, which, like our letter *lamed*, comes from the root word *lamad*. According to Strong's lexicon, *lamad* means "to goad; by implication to *teach* (the rod being an incentive)."

In the English Bible, the word *lamad*, or some form of *lamad*, is translated as "accustom, diligent, expert, instruct, learn, skillful, teach, teacher, teaching." From this same word, *lamad*, we get two other well-known Hebrew words: *Talmud* (the vast body of rabbinic teaching) and *talmid* (a student).

In biblical times, an ox goad could be as much as eight feet in length. One end was blunt; it served as a handle and as a means of removing the soil from the plow share. The other end had a sharp metal point to it. The pointed end served to "encourage" and motivate the oxen to go in the right direction.

In getting domesticated animals such as cows and sheep to obey, herdsmen have sometimes achieved a measure of control over the animals by spoken commands alone. There have been cases where a shepherd has given names to individual sheep that he has worked with over a long period, and when he calls one sheep by its name, that particular sheep has been known to respond.

Although such familiarity between herdsman and animal is the ideal, the *average* ox or sheep always remains at the level where such helpful aids as sheepdogs, fences, rods, ox goads, and that ultimate means — the rope — must be employed. This makes a great deal of sense. Humans have the power of speech and communicate with words, but it is unrealistic for people to expect animals to understand our speech (especially at first).

Therefore, we communicate with animals by means they can readily understand, such as ox goads. When the ox is jabbed by the ox goad for the first time, his master has gained his attention, and that is all. But after a few encounters with that pointed goad, the ox begins to form an opinion about such an implement! Eventually, the ox can be maneuvered by the very *sight* of the goad, and does not require constant prodding.

When we understand that this goad represents the Word of God, we can easily see the comparison as it relates to us, the flock of His pasture!

Often there is a sharp quality to God's Word. Have you ever read a beautiful scripture which describes the kind of good heart attitude or heart response that God desires, only to be painfully made aware, upon examining your heart, that you are nowhere near where you want to be?

Through such instances, the Word prods us — even jabs us — in order to motivate, encourage, and direct us to go in the right way. Eventually, however, when we know what the Master desires us to do, we do not require the frequent reminding of the pointed stick.

We are completely motivated (through previous instruction) to serve and please Him. We have *learned*. Again, we emphasize that the verb "learn" *(lamad)* is the root of *lamed*, our ox goad letter. If an ox can learn, how much more should we!

In this vein, let us examine a pertinent truth from Psalm 32:8,9. In these two verses are contrasted two kinds of people with whom the Lord deals in two different ways.

In verse 8, we find those who have been instructed by the Lord to such a degree that His eye alone is necessary to guide them: "I will instruct you and teach you in the way which you shall go; I will guide you with my eye."

As a loving father's children seated around the dinner table know whether their actions are making him happy or sad simply by seeing the expression in his eyes, those who intimately know the nature and laws of their Father in heaven can be guided by His very *eye;* that is, His expression. They have become familiar with their Father's face!

Contrasted with such well-trained believers are those of the next verse, who are like stubborn animals which can only be guided by means of bit and bridle: "Do not be like the horse or the mule, who have no understanding, who must be controlled with bit and bridle, or they will not come to you."

Is it not much better for us to voluntarily fill our hearts with God's Word and let Him guide us with His eye, rather than to require a bit, bridle, goad, or rod to induce us to do what is merely our duty? Yes, the goad does have a sharp point to it, and this is so we may be trained to do what is right naturally.

How do we know that the goad may be equated with the word of instruction? Ecclesiastes 12:11,12 (paraphrased) makes the connection in a clear way: "The words of the wise are like goads, and like firmly embedded nails given by one Shepherd. Be warned, my son, of anything in addition to them."

So there we have it: God's eternal Word, which Jesus our Shepherd perfectly embodies, instructs and corrects us, goads us, motivates us, and steers us in the right direction.

Saul experienced the sharp goading of the Lord. He had thoroughly learned the scriptures, and while he was persecuting the believers, those very scriptures troubled his conscience.

The Lord knew well that Saul was battling the divine prodding. When the blinding light knocked Saul to the ground, the Lord spoke these words from heaven: "Saul, Saul, why are you persecuting me? ...I am Jesus, whom you are persecuting. It is hard for you to kick against the goads" (Acts 9:4,5).

It *was* difficult for Saul to kick against the goad of God's law, prophets, and writings. This divine goad is even sharper than the one with which Shamgar (Israel's deliverer in Judges 3:31) slew 600 Philistines, men who were Israel's vehement enemies.

God's Word in the hands of His champion penetrates to the very heart of all human problems and stirs our wills to serve God wholeheartedly.

Lamed is the Word of God, the most capable goad and motivator of all. This goad was skillfully applied by Jesus while on Earth, is being applied now, and will realize its universal purpose when He returns to reign. Then, under King Jesus, "out of Zion shall go forth the law, and the word of the Lord from Jerusalem" (Isaiah 2:3).

(*Pronounced MEM*)

Chapter 13
Mem: Water or Waves

Technical Data: Mem is the thirteenth letter of the Hebrew alphabet. More than 1,030 words in the Hebrew Bible begin with the letter *mem*. Of these, 220 are proper names and places, and 810 are regular words. The Greek equivalent of *mem* is *mu*. Our English letter is "m."

Jewish Definitions: Some Jewish writers spiritualize the word *mem* as two kinds of waters, the accessible and the inaccessible. Because the word starts with an open *mem*, the word is indicative of the lower waters accessible to us, like oceans, lakes, rivers and ponds. The word ends with a closed *mem*. Alluding to Genesis 1:7, the writers infer that the nature of the upper waters is beyond our comprehension and is closed to us, like the final *mem*.

Christian Definitions: Most writers consulted call *mem* "water." Gesenius does add the word "waves." John MacMillan notes that water is used for cleansing and quenches the thirst. Strong's adds that figuratively, the word could include "juice." Jeremiah 2:13 speaks of the Lord as a fountain of living waters.

63

Devotional Comments

The thirteenth letter, *mem*, represents "water." The Hebrew word for "water" is *mayim*, a word with a plural ending. To English speakers, the word "water" is singular, although we sometimes say "waters" when discussing seas or some combination of bodies of water.

However, in looking at something so confined as water in a glass, we must admit that we are unable to pinpoint where one part of the water ends and another part begins. The entire glassful might as well be "waters," since it all mixes together. So in this chapter we shall use "water" or "waters," whichever best expresses the thought in English.

The word *mayim* occurs nearly 600 times in the Old Testament. There are also numerous scriptural references to rivers, streams, seas, waves, floods, wells, springs, rain, snow, hail, ice, clouds, dew, and mist. There are another 90 references to the word "water" in the New Testament.

Because this subject is so important in scripture, it is quite difficult to comment on it in a brief manner. The subject is made even more complex by several recurring biblical themes concerning water.

Frequent mention is made of raging waters out of control. There are references to tempestuous waves of the sea and to the floods of ungodly men. Sometimes the "seas" are given to mean the raging heathen nations. There are also "the waters of adversity."

In the Song of Songs, we find that the waters and floods of adversity can neither drown nor quench true love. In both Testaments we have references to the waters of washing or purifying, which is called the baptism in the New Testament.

Most often, water is used in a highly positive sense in scripture. In some portions of the Promised Land, water is nearly as valuable as gold. Because water is of utmost necessity for livestock, gardening, farming, and drinking, much effort goes into securing an adequate water supply.

For example, Isaac, in his adult life, seems to be famous mainly as a man who dug a lot of wells! Wells are, of course, fed by rainwater which has seeped into the ground over a period of time.

Rain is almost always considered *a blessing* in scripture, and the lack of rain is *a calamity.* (See "showers of blessing," Ezekiel 34:26.)

Several passages equate righteousness with the security of life-giving water. Psalm 1:3 compares a righteous man to a tree securely planted beside rivers of water. This tree bears fruit regularly and has leaves that never die.

An almost identical description of the man who trusts and hopes in the Lord is given in Jeremiah 17:7,8. Another magnificent verse is Isaiah 58:11, which says, "The Lord will guide you continually, and will satisfy your soul in drought...and you will be like a well-watered garden, like a spring whose waters never fail."

Another such verse is Isaiah 66:12. The Lord had been speaking of the coming consolation of Jerusalem, and He then declared, "Behold, I will extend peace to her like a river, and the glory of the nations like a flowing stream."

The theme which is most essential to this study is that of the "water of life." Everyone surely knows that water is an absolute necessity for the preservation of human life. A healthy person might go without eating for almost six weeks, but he cannot go without water for three days.

Some understanding of the importance of water is given to us by the Creator as we consider two of His most magnificent works: the Earth and the human body.

It is a truth of scripture that God fashioned the Earth to be inhabited by the "sons of men." (See Psalm 115:16 and Isaiah 45:18.) Yet the Earth's surface, every square mile being theoretically a place for people to reside, is less than one-third dry land! The remainder is water.

The oceans of the world make the land areas fit for habitation, balancing Earth's temperatures and providing varying degrees of rainfall around the globe. Similarly, the human body, which we regard as "solid" flesh, is approximately 80 percent water!

These two examples alone show us the significance of water. But when the scriptures speak of the water of life, something much more essential is meant than merely the fluid which we drink. What is spoken of is the life-giving sustenance of the Lord God Almighty! In fact, the Lord proclaims that He *is* the Fountain of Living Waters.

In Jeremiah 2:13, the Lord is speaking of the way that His people forsake and neglect Him: "My people have committed two evils; they have forsaken me the fountain of living waters, and have dug their own cisterns, broken cisterns, that cannot hold water."

Tragically, God's people have often refused the permanent satisfaction that comes from drinking at the divine well in favor of drinking out of some flimsy container of their own devising — only to end up thirsty and discontented.

Nevertheless, the Lord holds out the invitation for all to come and drink deeply of the only thing that can fully satisfy a person — a true relationship with the Lord God. "Whoever is thirsty let him come. And whoever wishes, let him take the free gift of the water of life" (Revelation 22:17). Since the Lord is the source and supply of all that is good, everything that surrounds His presence is flourishing and full of vitality.

There is a tremendous verse in Isaiah which speaks of the glory that the Lord will show forth when He is present among His people. Again it compares the Lord to rivers of water:

> For there [in Jerusalem] the glorious Lord will be unto us a place of broad rivers and streams; no galley with oars will ride them, no mighty ship will sail them.
>
> For the Lord is our Judge, the Lord is our Lawgiver, the Lord is our King; it is He who will save us.
>
> Isaiah 33:21,22 author's paraphrase

66

In the New Testament we see how the Lord Jesus promised a well-spring of life to those who follow Him. In John 4:13,14 *(NIV)*, Jesus told the Samaritan woman at Jacob's well:

Everyone who drinks this water will be thirsty again, but whoever drinks the water I give him will never thirst. Indeed, the water I give him will become in him a spring of water welling up to eternal life.

Compare to John 6:35: "...he who believes in me will never be thirsty."

The Feast of Tabernacles, known as *Succot* in Hebrew, holds special significance in the ministry of Jesus. The final day of *Succot* is the seventh day of the feast, and it is called *Hoshanah Rabbah,* the great Hosanna.

On this particular day, the priests would stand in the Temple courts and earnestly beseech God to send rain for the coming season. At a certain point, they poured out a container of water upon the ground, signifying that the prayers had been received.

Rejoicing, singing, dancing, and shouting broke out spontaneously. Writers who lived during the Second Temple Period state that whoever has not observed the rejoicing in Jerusalem during the Feast of Tabernacles has never seen rejoicing at all!

It was on *Hoshanah Rabbah* that Jesus made His great announcement at the Temple, in John 7:37,38 *(NIV)*:

On the last and greatest day of the Feast, Jesus stood and said in a loud voice, "If anyone is thirsty, let him come to me, and drink.

"Whoever believes in me, as the Scripture has said, streams of living water will flow from within him."

As one ponders this verse and the story of the woman at Jacob's well, the meaning becomes clear: Jesus is the Giver of the waters of life. As we are united with Him, we can have a supply of living water (the joys of salvation, peace, contentment, wholeness, holiness, the gifts of the Holy Spirit, everlasting life) within us, which will flow out and bless other people.

The ultimate description of the waters of life is given in Revelation 7:15-17 *(New American Standard Bible)*:

> ...they are before the throne of God; and they serve Him day and night in His temple; and He who sits on the throne shall spread His tabernacle over them.

> They shall hunger no more, neither thirst any more; neither shall the sun beat down on them, nor any heat;

> for the Lamb in the center of the throne shall be their shepherd, and shall guide them to springs of the water of life; and God shall wipe every tear from their eyes.

Who can fathom the peace, contentment, and unhindered joy that shall be ours as we continue to follow our Messiah in an eternal relationship of love?

Mem is the satisfying, thirst-quenching water of life which Jesus promised to give us!

(*Pronounced NOON*)

Chapter 14
Nun: Fish

Technical Data: Nun is the fourteenth letter of the Hebrew alphabet, and 435 words in the Hebrew Bible start with *nun.* Of these, 91 are proper names and places, and 344 are regular words. The Greek equivalent is *nu.* Our English letter is "n."

Jewish Definitions: One Jewish writer called attention to Jacob's blessing Joseph's children by using a spawning term *(dagah).* He proclaimed that they will multiply prolifically, like fish!

The word *nun* or "fish" denotes productiveness. Rashi adds the thought "just as fish under water are concealed from the sight of others, so would Jacob's descendants be protected from malevolent eyes even though they live on Earth, exposed to envy."

Christian Definitions: All the sources consulted defined *nun* as "fish." John MacMillan did mention that *ichthus,* the Greek word for "fish," was the most ancient symbol of the Christian faith. *Strong's Concordance* defines *nun* as "resprouting, propagating by shoots, or to continue in perpetuity."

Devotional Comments

Letter 14 is *nun*, and it signifies a fish. There are about 37 references to fish and fishing in the Old Testament, and about 33 such references in the New Testament.

Fishing as a livelihood dates from very ancient times. Many different cultures were aware of the value of fish, which we now know to be a remarkably nutritious food.

It is a wonderful fact of geography that Israel is situated in a perfect place at the conjunction of the three major Old World continents. The Bible describes the land of Canaan as a land flowing with milk and honey, a land full of delight, the most pleasant of all lands, and a land for which the Lord God cares.

He *does* care for His unique land in a manner which goes beyond His general care for all the Earth. By the wisdom through which He designed the Promised Land — with some areas of lengthy growing seasons, and with rainfall amounts ranging from heavy to light — all kinds of produce flourishes for the benefit of His blessed people.

The land was set up and established to feed His children, and their righteousness would insure the continuation of the good life that the land was designed to provide. Because of this, we can understand how the Lord mourned over His people's ways in Psalm 81:13,14,16:

> **Oh that my people had hearkened unto me, and Israel had walked in my ways!**
>
> **How quickly would I subdue their enemies, and turn my hand against their foes....**
>
> **[Israel] would be fed with the finest of wheat; with honey from the rock I would satisfy you.**

God's desire has always been to feed His people with the finest food, both spiritually and physically. As a further illustration of the advantageous situation of the Promised Land, we cite the following lesser-known facts:

Hundreds of millions of fish spend the winter in the Atlantic Ocean off the western coast of Africa. In the springtime, they head up the coast toward the Strait of Gibraltar. Although this opening to the Mediterranean Sea is quite narrow, it is very deep.

For reasons not fully known, the great majority of these fish do not continue to go up the coast toward Portugal; instead, they pass through the Strait of Gibraltar into the Mediterranean. Then, swept along the coast of North Africa by currents, the fish must turn North (as does the coastline) past the delta of the Nile. As they pass by the coast of Southwest Asia (Israel and Lebanon), they become candidates for local meals! Not until the surviving fish pass Cyprus do they split up into groups of various species, seeking places to spawn.

Thus, the people in Bible times were acquainted with a large variety of fish. *It is as if God designed a great, rotating table in the sea to sweep in front of Israel for the nourishment of His elect nation!*

Who can fail to see the kindness and the provision of the Lord in these things? He fed them with the finest wheat, the finest oil, the finest produce — and the finest fish, brought in from the Atlantic Ocean!

The most important fish in the Bible is, of course, the "great fish" God prepared for Jonah, and this is also the most important fish in our study.

Jonah was swallowed by a great fish and remained in its belly for three days and three nights. He finally emerged from the fish alive — which was a miracle — and preached his message of repentance to a large Gentile audience in Nineveh, which is where God sent him in the first place. (Please read the entire Book of Jonah for the history of these events.)

At this point, we wish to clarify the biblical words used to describe Jonah's fish. In the Book of Jonah, the word *dag* is used, which is the Hebrew word normally used to mean "fish." There are other Hebrew words which could suggest great sea creatures, but it was the word *dag* which was used.

In the New Testament, the word *kaytos* is used, which means "a huge fish, gaping for prey." The word *kaytos* itself comes from a certain form of the word *chasma* (from which we get our word "chasm"), meaning "a gulf, a vacancy, or an impassable interval." *Chasma* comes from *chao*, which means "to gape or yawn."

So to be faithful to the text, we see that *it is a gaping, yawning, huge fish that the Bible describes.* (It is true that in some of our English versions, the word "whale" was chosen to try to define the "fish" that Jonah encountered, but as has been stated, the original scriptures all say it was a "fish," and so shall we.)

Jesus spoke about Jonah, his experience in the fish, and his preaching, which caused the citizens of Nineveh to repent. He laid a great deal of importance on the significance of Jonah's experience and said that the only sign (*oth* in Hebrew, meaning "a signal, beacon, monument, omen, evidence, proof, or token") His generation would be given was the sign of the prophet Jonah.

In Matthew 12:38-41, when some of the religious authorities desired a miraculous sign from Jesus (perhaps the healing of multitudes of people, which was witnessed publicly, or the fact that Jesus never lost any dispute with anyone in the scriptures was not sign enough), He responded:

A wicked and adulterous generation asks for a miraculous sign. But none will be given to it except the sign of the prophet Jonah.

For as Jonah was three days and three nights in the belly of a huge fish, so the Son of Man will be three days and three nights in the heart of the earth.

The men of Nineveh will stand up at the judgment with this generation and condemn it; for they *repented* at the preaching of Jonah, and now a greater than Jonah is here.

Matthew 12:39-41

This tremendous passage points to the Resurrection and to a greater ministry than that of Jonah. If being swallowed alive by a huge fish is the end of all reasonable hope for life, dying and being buried is a more unchangeable circumstance!

When Jonah was brought up out of the fish alive, it was both a miracle and a sign that God was with him. When Jesus came up out of the gates of death, it was a greater miracle and a greater sign that God was with Him! As Jonah's greatest effect on society came *after* his release from the fish's belly, so Jesus' most profound effect on the whole world came after His Resurrection.

As Jonah was instructed by God to take his message of repentance to a Gentile civilization, so Jesus' apostles were instructed by the Lord to take the good news of repentance and salvation to all nations!

In short, *the greatest testimony that the Lord God was pleased with Jesus and His mission was simply that He raised Him from the dead!*

He had done no violence, neither was any deceit in his mouth.

Yet it was the Lord's will to crush him and cause him to suffer, and though the Lord makes his life a guilt offering, he will see his offspring and prolong his days, and the pleasure of the Lord shall prosper in his hand.

By his knowledge my righteous servant shall justify many, and he will bear their iniquities.

Therefore I will give him a portion among the great, and he will divide the spoils with the strong, *because* he poured out his life unto death, and was numbered with the transgressors.

Isaiah 53:9-12

God endorsed Jesus' holy labor by raising Him up. God told Moses:

I will *raise up* a Prophet like you from among their brothers; I will put my words in his mouth, and he will tell them everything I command him.

If anyone does not listen to my words that the Prophet speaks in my name, I myself will call him to account.

Deuteronomy 18:18,19

Many prophets were "raised up" in the sense that they were sent to minister in a particular generation, but none of them was ever put to death and then raised up by God except this one Prophet which Moses foretold — Jesus Himself!

The New Testament doctrine which unbelieving people are most tempted to try to disprove is the Resurrection of Jesus. Yet it was impossible to deny it in Jerusalem, where hundreds of people at a time had been eyewitnesses that Jesus was alive again, and these people who saw Him had *known* Him before His death!

The explanations and excuses for what might have actually occurred could almost be humorous if they were not so pathetic. Even so, people find it easier to try to deny this miracle sign of Jesus' ministry today than did the unbelieving inhabitants of Jerusalem *at the time it occurred!*

Nun is the fish that portrays the greatest miracle: The prophet was swallowed up, but he came out alive to fulfill his destiny! That is to say, the Prophet (Jesus) was swallowed up by death and the grave, but God raised Him up; He emerged alive; and repentance was preached everywhere in His name. *This is a proof that He was the One sent from God.*

It is interesting that the earliest believers in Jesus used only one symbol to identify themselves, and that was the outline of a fish. More curious is the fact that the word *ichthus,* which is "fish" in Greek, is an acronym for the following Greek words: *Iesus CHristos THeou Uios Soter,* meaning "Jesus (the) Messiah, God's Son, Savior."

In times of dire persecution, believers throughout the entire Greek-speaking world used this simple sign (the sign of the fish, representing the "sign" of the prophet Jonah) to reveal themselves to each other.

It may come as a surprise to you that it was not until much later (when the Church had fallen into many forms of darkness) that a cross was used as a symbol of faith. The earliest believers were known by the symbol of Resurrection, not the symbol of death! They had, therefore, a proper emphasis on the ministry of our greater-than-Jonah.

Jesus Himself announced, "I am the living One; I was dead, and behold I am alive for ever and ever! And I hold the keys of death and hades" (Revelation 1:18).

When we see *nun*, the fish, we think of the sign of the prophet Jonah — the Resurrection of Jesus!

(Pronounced SAH-MEKH)

Chapter 15

Samech: **Prop or Support**

Technical Data: Samech is the fifteenth letter of the Hebrew alphabet. Of the 216 words in the Hebrew Bible starting with the letter *samech*, 55 are proper name and places, and 161 are regular words. The Greek equivalent is *xi* (*ksee*, as in "taxi"). Our English letter would be "s."

Jewish Definitions: A Jewish writer said that *samech* is a symbol of support, protection, and memory. On the active side of *samech* is God providing support. On the passive side of *samech* is man relying on God. Our memory serves to remind us of our constant reliance upon the Lord.

Christian Definitions: "Prop and support" is the major consensus of *samech*. John MacMillan did add that the ministry of helps or "helpers" comes from this word. James Strong defines *samech* as "to lean upon, to take hold of, to sustain and to stay oneself." Isaiah 26:3 is a good example of *samech:* "Thou wilt keep him in perfect peace, whose mind is stayed [*samech*] or propped up, or leaning on the Lord."

Devotional Comments

Samech, the fifteenth letter of the Hebrew alphabet, means "a prop or support." This suggests something that may be leaned upon, such as a staff.

There are eight different Hebrew words for "staff" in the Bible. All of us are familiar with the shepherd's staff — the staff he leaned upon.

In the universally acclaimed Twenty-Third Psalm, we find our Divine Shepherd's rod and staff to be a comfort to us. The patriarch Jacob took only his staff when he walked from Canaan to Padan-aram in search of a wife (Genesis 32:10).

Many years later at the end of his life, he worshipped in thankfulness while leaning on his staff, or on the bed post. (See Genesis 47:31; Hebrews 11:21.)

The children of Israel were told to have their staffs in their hands on the night of departure from Egypt: "This is how you are to eat [the Passover meal]: with your cloak tucked into your belt, your sandals on your feet, and your staff in your hand. Eat it in haste; it is the Lord's Passover" (Exodus 12:11).

In other words, they were getting ready to march! A staff was useful for people of all ages as they set out toward the rugged Sinai wilderness. Aided by a good staff, a person can gain surefootedness in walking.

Of course, there are more props and supports in the Bible than staffs alone. In the Prophets, we find that God's people were often rebuked for their tragic tendency to lean on Egypt or Assyria rather than to wholeheartedly trust in the Lord God of Israel.

Sometimes these nations themselves acknowledged their unreliability. In Second Kings 18:21, an Assyrian commander stood outside Jerusalem's walls and taunted its citizens with these pointed words: "Look now, you that are depending on Egypt, that splintered reed of a staff, which pierces a man's hand and wounds him if he leans on it! Such is Pharaoh King of Egypt to all who depend on him."

Since these flimsy supports were so untrustworthy, they always hurt and disappointed those who leaned on them. There is a real lesson in these unhappy experiences. It seems that one of the fatal flaws of human beings everywhere is that, given the opportunity, we tend much rather to put our trust in people, organizations, or even ourselves than in the Maker of us all. This foolish bent has caused most of the heartache we find in the world.

Perhaps it is of great significance that the very middle verse of the whole Bible is Psalm 118:8, which expresses a central truth in the Bible: "It is better to trust in the Lord than to put confidence in man."

Most societies have this unchangeable priority reversed — God is not considered capable of any help, and all trust and confidence is put in the undependable, self-contradictory, unstable human being and his capabilities!

If anything is doomed to failure it is leaning on unregenerate people rather than being supported by the everlasting arms of the God of Israel and being held securely in the Messiah's arms!

The eternal God is your refuge, and underneath are the everlasting arms.

Deuteronomy 33:27

He tends his flock like a shepherd: he gathers the lambs in his arms and carries them close to his heart; he gently leads those that have young.

Isaiah 40:11

It is a proven principle that when we reject the good that God is seeking to give us, we may get something instead which makes us very unhappy. One of the prime biblical examples of this is the tragedy of Saul, Israel's first king.

When the people demanded that the conscientious judge Samuel should provide a king for them, God told Samuel, "The people have not rejected you, but they have rejected *Me*, that I should not be king over them."

God went on to instruct Samuel to give the people their hearts' desire in a king, and in the process to warn them that their king would become so oppressive they would become as his slaves! "When that day comes, you will cry out for relief from the king *you* have chosen, but the Lord will not answer you in that day!" This account is found in First Samuel 8:1-22.

Saul was the people's first king, and he started out very successfully. God, however, knowing the hearts of all men, allowed the people to have Saul as their king in order to illustrate the difference between man's choice and God's choice.

Saul became proud, and then jealous, insecure, and hostile. He deteriorated into a state of mental illness that was characterized by fits of rage and threats against his family and servants.

He tried to kill God's beloved servant David on 21 occasions! He became so insane that he murdered an entire city of the Lord's priests, killing men, women, *and infants,* because he mistakenly thought they were loyal to David! On one occasion, the people had to physically prevent Saul from murdering his own son Jonathan, the only decent member of his family!

When Saul's servants did not reveal where David was hiding, Saul went into a childish fit of self-pity, according to First Samuel 22:7,8: "Listen men...will the son of Jesse give all of you fields and vineyards? Will he make all of you commanders of thousands? Is that why you have all conspired against *me?* No one tells *me* when my son makes a covenant with the son of Jesse. None of you is concerned about *me* or tells *me* that my son has incited my servant to lie in wait for *me* as he does today!"

In the insanity of his paranoid state, Saul was imagining that his victims were his tormentors, and he was falsely accusing David, Jonathan, and the servants. In his sick, self-centered way he resorted to the old "nobody cares about me" routine.

Saul finally made himself so repulsive that God would no longer answer him! He then turned to the occult, hoping to hear from someone — anyone. He spent his final evening in the company of a witch! The following day he led Israel to defeat on the mountains of Gilboa, and he committed suicide in despair.

Saul has gone down in history as a most egomaniacal, self-exalting, destructive person. All he cared about was holding onto his position of power and control, so he lost it all!

After Israel was humbled through these grievous events, God brought out His choice — David, a man after His own heart. All David cared about was his lifelong desire to love and praise God. (See Psalm 27:4-6.)

The Lord did not express any words of tribute to His first anointed king, Saul. He only said, "I have rejected him." Ironically, the only tribute we have to Saul was the beautiful poem composed in his honor by *David!*

But when David died after a life full of loving praises to God, he was given a stunning tribute in First Kings 11:4,6, where it is recorded that David's heart was perfect with the Lord his God, and he followed the Lord completely.

By human standards, Saul, who was a foot taller than any other man in Israel, should have been the desirable king; and David, who was the youngest and smallest of seven brothers, should have been an unlikely candidate to make the Kingdom of Israel greater than it was before or after. History has vindicated God's choice.

There is a greater David who is also God's choice. He came in the authority of the Holy One and was the rightful heir to David's throne. He desired only to do those things that please the Father. His motives were pure.

The night before He laid down His life, He said, "Father, I have glorified You on the Earth." His nation contained many devout men who were righteous and upright, but none of them was able to say, "I have made the Lord glorious on the Earth."

81

Jesus was the Father's choice. Jesus of Nazareth was, is, and always shall be God's only Messiah, and human rejection can never change God's mind concerning the One He sent.

As we have noted, *Jesus was the only voice in His time to accurately predict the last 1,900 years of Jewish history,* specifying the destruction of the Temple by the Romans, the fall of Judea, the captivity of the Jewish people among the Gentiles, the ingathering of the exiles, and the possession of Jerusalem in our day — thus describing in sequence what *we must acknowledge has happened in this precise order!*

Having so clear a picture of the national tragedy about to occur, He had an equally clear insight into the spiritual void which the rejection of the one true Messiah would produce. He predicted a time that people would even desperately grasp at false messiahs whose motives were selfish and who were never sent from God at all:

> There shall arise false messiahs, and false prophets, and shall perform great signs and miracles, insomuch that, if it were possible, they shall deceive the elect — God's chosen ones.
>
> **Matthew 24:24**

> I have come in my Father's name and with His power, and you do not receive me. But if another comes in his own name and his own power, with no other authority but himself, you will receive him, and give him your approval.
>
> **John 5:43**

What a fulfillment these two statements of Jesus have seen! He said that many false messiahs would come, and there have been at least 40 such men who appeared with promises of Redemption, but ultimately they spread much grief and harm among the Jewish communities. Jesus said that such self-authorized men would be received and approved, and thus it has been.

One such man was Simeon Bar Kokba, leader of the final Jewish revolt against Rome in the second century. Claiming descent from David, and having the noted Rabbi Akiba's endorsement ("This is King Messiah"), Bar Kokba set out to throw off the Roman yoke and liberate Judea.

Initially successful, Bar Kokba was finally killed by Hadrian's forces, as were 580,000 other Jews. Many survivors were sold as slaves.

As a consequence of the Bar Kokba Revolt, the Roman Empire, which was still pagan, instituted fierce anti-Jewish restrictions against keeping the Sabbath, circumcision, and studying the Torah. To add insult to injury, the Romans even prohibited Jews from setting foot in Jerusalem!

Bar Kokba, the unfortunate would-be liberator of Israel, was held responsible by posterity for so grievously aggravating the disaster that had already befallen the Jewish nation in the year A.D. 70.

After Bar Kokba's revolt, all opportunity for national restoration was lost for nearly 18 centuries! Because of the unhappy outcome, Patriarch Rabbi Judah I infers that Bar Kokba's actual name, Ben Koziba, means "son of lies"; that is to say, false promises.

Nearly 580,000 people perished while leaning on this man who called himself the "Star out of Jacob" mentioned in Numbers 24:17. But prior to this, of those people who had heeded Jesus' explicit instructions in Luke 21:20-22 concerning when to flee from Jerusalem, *not one lost his life!*

History records that there were only 1,500 persons who remembered and acted on these warnings Jesus gave concerning the fall of Jerusalem. The people who relied on Him were relying on the One whose words have proved to be true. But the *numbers* — 1,500 compared to 580,000 who trusted Bar Kokba — are so distressing and heartbreaking!

The most famous false Messiah was Shabbetai Zevi (1626-1676), who first revealed himself in the year 1648 at Smyrna as "the true Messianic redeemer designated by God to overthrow the governments of the nations and to restore Israel to Jerusalem." (See *Jewish Encyclopedia*, volume XI, pages 218-225.)

In the following 17 years, Zevi's fame spread throughout Europe, Africa, and Asia. In 1665 he went to Jerusalem with his right-hand man, Nathan of Gaza, who claimed to be the prophet Elijah, and who announced that the Messianic Age would begin the following year.

As was expected, Shabbetai was publicly declared Messiah in the synagogue of Smyrna in 1666 with the blowing of horns and shouts of "Long live our King, our Messiah!" He then sent out the following proclamation to the entire Jewish world:

The first-begotten Son of God, Shabbetai Zevi, Messiah and redeemer of the people of Israel, to all the sons of Israel, peace! Since ye have been deemed worthy to behold the great day and the fulfillment of God's words by the prophets, your lament and sorrow must be changed into joy, and your fasting into merriment, for ye shall weep no more. Rejoice with song and melody, and change the day formerly spent in sadness and sorrow into a day of jubilee, because I have appeared.

Although Shabbetai was renounced by many Jews, including a number of conscientious rabbis, his appeal was so great in some parts of Europe that people began to unroof their homes in preparation for the exodus to Palestine, and 17th century prayer books printed in Germany and Holland contained this prayer: "Bless our Lord and King, the holy and the righteous Shabbetai Zevi, the Messiah of the God of Jacob."

At the height of expectation of promised deliverance, Shabbetai's followers were stunned by the news that the Turkish Sultan Mohammed IV had imprisoned Zevi and threatened him with death if he would not convert to Islam. So Shabbetai Zevi became a Muslim in order to save his life!

Banished to an obscure Albanian village, Zevi died as a lonely man in exile. The immediate harm which followed his death was the grief and shame caused to his hundreds of thousands of embarrassed followers, some of whom were rabbis. Yet there were two much more injurious backlashes which we must consider.

First, the leadership of the Shabbetaian Movement adopted the doctrine that Messiah must *sin* in order to bring Redemption. This was an attempt to justify as part of the "messianic scheme" Zevi's embrace of Islam. As years passed, this corrupt teaching further deteriorated into the concept that the more sin one commits in order to bring Redemption, the greater the Redemption will be!

The final successor to the Shabbetaians was Jacob Frank (1726-1791), who was responsible for a world of evil himself. As Rabbi Marvin Antelman has so thoroughly shown in his well-researched book *To Eliminate the Opiate*, the end result of the Shabbetaian-Frankist Movement was an organized movement in Germany for the destruction of the Bible and the elimination of Judaism and Christianity from Europe.

Furthermore, those who built upon the combined tenets of the Frankists and the Biblical Destruction League contributed to the physical destruction of Europe's Jews in this century. This is like the sting of a scorpion, and is a fearful tragedy!

The second backlash is more subtle but equally tragic. The legacy left by Shabbetai Zevi (and other impostors before him) was so damaging that the rabbis felt the need to exercise extreme caution whenever "visionaries" suggested a mass return to Zion.

Equating the proposed 20th century emigration from Europe with the false messianic hysteria of past centuries, a certain number of overly cautious rabbis made their greatest mistake in modern times: *the rejection of Zionism.*

When Theodore Herzl and the World Jewish Congress presented their sensible plans for the proposed Jewish State, it sounded to many people like a repeat of elusive hopes of past movements. Perhaps the most hostile words ever directed against Zionism were those spoken and written by rabbis! (See *Jewish Encyclopedia*, Volume XII, pages 673-674.)

They did not recognize Zionism as a part of God's merciful leading of His scattered flock to safety and independence. Zionism was the only sure escape from the mass annihilation of Europe's Jews in the Nazi holocaust, yet many rabbis discouraged their trusting congregations from having anything to do with Herzl.

Those who did not have the insight, yearning, or ability to *leave* Europe before the doors were finally closed were left defenseless to face the largest, most criminal mass slaughter in the history of the world! Had it not been for self-seeking, dishonorable men such as Zevi, more credibility would certainly have been given to such honorable men as Herzl. This is a *compound misfortune.*

As this book is meant to honor the true Messiah, actual biographies of false messiahs would be out of place. However, we might suggest that those who desire an enlightening study on the topic do research under the following names: Abraham Abulafia, David Alroy, Simeon Bar Kokba, Menahem Ben Judah, Chaim Vital Calabrese, Miguel Cardoso, Isaiah Chasid (who claimed to be the resurrected Shabbetai Zevi), Jonathan Eybeschutz, Jacob Frank, Nathan Ghazzati, Abu Isa Isfahani, Asher Lemmlein, Isaac Luria, Moses Luzzatto, Mordecai Mokiach, and Solomon Molko.

Moses of Crete, a fifth century false messiah, promised to part the sea and lead his followers to Palestine. He persuaded them to cast themselves into the sea from a cliff, and many drowned, although some were rescued by passing sailors.

Other false messiahs were: Lobele Prossnitz, Jacob Zevi Querido (who was regarded as the incarnation of Shabbetai Zevi), Berechiah Ben Jacob Querido, Yudgan al Rai, David Reubeni, Serene, Abraham Shalom, Shabbetai Zevi, and others of the Donmeh sect.

When Jesus said, "If another comes in his own name, you will receive him," was He not foreseeing this succession of deceivers who sowed grief, shame, and disappointment in their bewildered followers?

These men preyed on the legitimate messianic yearnings of the scattered nation — longings which were expressed in the imploring prayer of the 11th century poet Ibn Gabirol: "Send a Prince to the condemned people which is scattered here and there."

But the false messiahs and deceivers could never *fulfill* the messianic needs of their people. They may have been to some extent the people's choice in their day, *but God's choice was required.*

Through the bitter disappointments brought on by these scores of deceivers, and through the final, most grievous betrayal by the ultimate anti-messiah, there will come a day when Israel will permanently be rid of any desire or even capacity to lean on any messiah other than God's choice — the One whose words have proved true, whose motives were pure, whose life glorified the Father, and who will yet rescue Israel from annihilation! There will be no urge to lean on any of these faulty "staffs" who have wounded those who leaned on them.

Isaiah foresaw the joyous day when this issue will be settled permanently in the hearts of his people. He prophesied in Isaiah 10:20, "In that day the remnant of Israel, the survivors of the House of Jacob, will no longer rely on him who struck them down, but will truly rely on the Lord, the Holy One of Israel."

Looking back over the 4,000 years from Abraham's time to the present day, we ask, "Who is so reliable, so sure, so trustworthy as to be leaned upon in truth?"

We have found our faithful support to be Jesus the Lord and Messiah — God's permanent choice!

Samech is the One who is the greatest support, prop, and help that a human being can have!

(Pronounced AH-YIN)

Chapter 16
Ayin: The Eye

Technical Data: The sixteenth letter of the Hebrew alphabet is *ayin,* and 639 words in the Hebrew Bible begin with *ayin.* Of these, 227 are proper names and places, and 412 are regular words.

The Greek equivalent of *ayin* is *omicron.* In ancient alphabets, *ayin* was represented by a circle. This was meant to represent the eye. The letter has changed form in time, but the eye definition has remained.

Ayin is the second of two Hebrew letters which have no equivalent English sound. It is a guttural aspirate sound, and although it is a distinct sound in Hebrew, it cannot be represented by any letter or combination of letters in English.

Jewish Definitions: Jewish writers say of *ayin,* "sight and insight." *Ayin* is the letter of perception and insight, for its name means "eye." *Ayin* also means "a spring of water." Rabbi Hirsch, quoting Genesis 3:5, states, "as a spring brings water from the dark depths to the light of the sun, so the eye brings the perception of the world into the human mind.

Through the narrow eye the entire universe is brought into focus."

Christian Definitions: By unanimous consensus, *ayin* is defined as "eye." Strong's does add "by analogy a fountain as the eye of the landscape." John MacMillan further states that *ayin* applies to seers as being men of vision.

There are cities in Israel beginning with the letters en, like Engedi, Endor, Enrogei, Engannim, Enhazor, and so forth. (More than 14 are thus named.) These names are *ayin* words, referring to the fountain or fountains in them. Just as tears come from the eyes, some scholars see wells as the eyes of mother earth weeping because of man's alienation from God.

An unusual look at *ayin* is found in First Samuel 16:7. "The Lord sees not as man sees. For man looks on the outward appearance [*ayin*], but the Lord looks on the heart." The only window to the soul we have is by the expression of the eyes.

Men try to do personality analysis by the eye-gate. That is all we have to go by. The Lord sees the inner condition and the heart condition. It is a more accurate reading. He knows the heart. All we can do is look at *ayin* — the eyes.

Devotional Comments

Our sixteenth letter, *ayin*, represents an eye. We are aware that the eye is one of the most intricately designed organs in the human body. The complexity of the eye may be demonstrated by comparing sight to hearing.

It only takes one nerve fiber to carry sound to the brain, in a similar way that a telephone conversation is carried through a single wire. Yet there are more than half a million nerve fibers by which the optic nerve carries visual pictures to the brain! But for all its intricacy, the eye alone does not guarantee that a person will have correct perception.

It is possible to see a picture clearly, yet be absolutely bewildered, disoriented, and unsure of what one is seeing. This is true of natural things as well as spiritual things. We must have the ability to correctly *interpret* what our eyes relay to us. For example, a person walking through a dense forest may not be able to differentiate between a branch and a snake, or between a leaf-covered rock and the opening to a deep pit.

We have all been fooled by camouflage and by mirages. Eventually, when your eyes are trained through experience, you know that not everything that looks like water on the road is actually water.

The eye has been called the window of the soul. It not only takes in the picture from the outside, but it can portray an accurate picture of what is inside as well. By the expression of one's eyes more than any other factor, we can usually ascertain anger, joy, kindness, sorrow, fatigue, and much more. When a person is lying, the pupils of the eye may behave in an irregular manner. As a result of a head injury, the pupils often become dilated. Above all, the eyes express the heart. When a person feels sorrow, loneliness, loss, relief, or intense gratitude, tears involuntarily pour forth from the eyes.

There are 600 biblical references to the word "eye" or "eyes." Naturally, we cannot examine all the various shades of meaning in these many references. Let us simply relate some verses which refer to God's all-perceiving eye.

The eyes of the Lord are in every place, beholding the evil and the good.

Proverbs 15:3

The eyes of the Lord run to and fro throughout the whole earth, to show Himself strong in the behalf of them whose heart is perfect toward Him.

2 Chronicles 16:9

The eyes of the Lord are upon the righteous, and His ears are open unto their cry.

Psalm 34:15

> **Nothing in all creation is hidden from God's sight. Every-
> thing is uncovered and laid bare before the eyes of Him to
> whom we must give account.**
>
> **Hebrews 4:13**

These scriptures portray the deep insight of the Lord
God into everything in the universe; even into the motives of
the human heart.

Such insight belonged to Jesus as He continually
revealed what was in the hearts and minds of those around
Him. Frequently it is recorded that Jesus perceived their
thoughts and knew what they were reasoning in their minds!

On one occasion, His disciples had been disputing as to
which one would be the greatest. When He asked them what
the cause of the dissension had been, they would not answer
Him. So without waiting for them to volunteer anything
about their rivalry, He answered their "unspoken request"
with these brief words: "If anyone wants to be first, he must
be the very last, and the servant of all" (Mark 9:35).

Jesus' sight went far beyond that which sight normally
encompasses. He *saw* Nathaniel sitting alone and secluded
from view beneath a fig tree. Then, when Jesus first met
Nathaniel, He said of him, "Here is a true Israelite in whom
there is nothing false."

Nathaniel asked, "How do you know me?"

Jesus answered, "I *saw* you while you were still under
the fig tree, before Philip called you."

Astonished by Jesus' ability to see and know what is
hidden, Nathaniel exclaimed, "Rabbi, you are the Son of God;
you are the King of Israel!" (John 1:47-49).

In this instance, Jesus had seen what was closed from
view because of the distance involved. In the following case
He saw what could not be seen by others due to the pro-
hibitive factor of time.

When the 70 disciples whom He had sent out were
rejoicing over their successes, He startled them with this
announcement: "I *saw* Satan fall from heaven." Although

this may have occurred before man was created, Jesus had clearly *seen* it. In the next example, Jesus saw what could not be seen by those who could not see beyond the offensiveness of a human personality.

A certain young rich man came running up to Jesus as though he only had a moment to ask Him a few questions. As they talked about the Ten Commandments, the young businessman told Jesus that he had observed all the Commandments from his youth. At that point, Jesus looked at the young man and *loved* him (Mark 10:21). He *saw* what most people who read this passage have yet to see — this young man was someone of great value in the Lord's eyes.

This same young man who went away completely unwilling to give up his excessive wealth to benefit the poor — this youth who has since been the subject of countless sermons — was seen by Jesus *as no one else could see him*. He saw past the young man's insecurities and selfishness to something in him that was commendable and worthy of being loved.

People who "see" a lot tend to weep a lot. People who find no occasion for tears in this world either cannot see at all, or they do not ponder what they can see.

Not so Jeremiah, the "weeping prophet," who wept so much because he saw the state of his people so clearly. He ministered for about 50 years and shed countless tears over the fate of his nation, which stood on the precipice of invasion and captivity — events which Jeremiah prophesied as clearly as Jesus did later when He foretold the coming disasters in Judea.

Jeremiah's vision was extraordinary, so his tears were profuse. But eventually he realized that he did not have the ability to shed *enough* tears to adequately lament the tragedies which he beheld. He wished for an increased source of water to supply his tears, even if his head must be hollowed out to form a cistern of water:

> **Oh that my head were waters, and mine eyes a fountain of tears, that I might weep day and night for the slain of the daughter of my people!**
>
> **Jeremiah 9:1**

He did not say, "Aha! I told you this would happen! For 50 years I've warned you stiff-necked citizens, but you didn't believe me," and so forth. No, he sat down amid the ruins and composed yet *another* lament, the Book of Lamentations, regarded as the most sorrowful poem contained in any literature in the world.

A true prophet of God who renounces the sin of the people must do so with weeping, as Jeremiah did. If a prophet can state the facts as God allows him to see them but not be moved to tears, there is something woefully lacking in him.

It is noteworthy that Jeremiah prophesied the desolation of Jerusalem and then lamented *after* it was destroyed; and Jesus prophesied the desolation of Jerusalem, but lamented over the city *before* it was destroyed.

> **As He approached Jerusalem and saw the city, He wept over it and said, "If you had only known what would bring you peace — but now it is hid from your eyes.**
>
> **"The days will come upon you when your enemies will build an embarkment against you and encircle you and hem you in on every side.**
>
> **"They will dash you to the ground, you and the children within your walls. They will not leave one stone on another, because you did not recognize the time of your visitation."**
>
> **Luke 19:41-44**

It is seldom noticed that when Jesus began His ministry and many were wondering who He could be, some people thought that He was one of the prophets come back to life; perhaps even *Jeremiah.* (See Matthew 16:14.) Why, out of all the prophets, did they identify Jeremiah with Jesus? Was it because He wept so much?

As we have seen, He wept over Jerusalem, and He also wept with "strong crying and tears" the night before His death. (Compare Hebrews 5:7 with Luke 22:44 and Mark 14:33-35.) And when His beloved friend Lazarus died, Jesus wept in such a manner that bystanders remarked, "Look at that! He must have loved him greatly."

Jesus stated that He never doubted that the Father would hear His prayer to raise Lazarus from the dead. But when He stood contemplating the death of His friend, and, indeed, death in general, His heart was flooded with all the distress, anger, sorrow, and grief that any other bereaved person feels. This sorrow is common to all peoples. When Jesus looked at the enemy called death, His heart was also broken, and He could not help but weep. Such was His love for people and His familiarity with our griefs.

Were the tears of the prophets, the martyrs, and those of the Messiah shed in vain? Did they somehow fall to the ground unnoticed and insignificant? Certainly not! David declared that the tears of the righteous should be put for safekeeping in God's bottle (Psalm 56:8). These priceless tears of godly men and women become as sweet as perfume in this bottle. They are also pictured as forming pools of water for the refreshment of those who would later came along the same path:

> **Blessed are those who, as they pass through the valley of weeping, make it a place of springs; the rain [of tears] also fills the pools.**
>
> **Psalm 84:6**

In God's miraculous way, these bitter, salty tears form pools of sweet water for others, as it is written, "Those who sow in tears shall reap in joy" (Psalm 126:5). Consider how the Psalmist was no stranger to tears: "My tears have been my food day and night, while they continually say to me, 'Where is your God?'" (Psalm 42:3).

Jesus was no stranger to tears, and because of what His eyes saw, His heart was troubled and His soul was burdened. Naturally, His eyes revealed the depth of wisdom and compassion which characterized His life and ministry.

The greatest, most life-changing sight at which a person can look is the face of Jesus the Messiah. To see Him, to look into His compassionate eyes as I did when 18 years of age, will forever leave the wonder and the majesty of His person engraved upon the heart and mind! What volumes Messiah's eyes speak! His eyes see more — see more deeply, see more clearly — than those of any other man.

Ayin is our Messiah's eyes, which have beheld everything. They have shed what to us may be uncountable tears, but God recorded and preserved every one of them and makes them into springs (*mayan*, which comes from our word *ayin*), fountains, wells, and pools for the sustenance of His people.

(*Pronounced PEY*)

Chapter 17
Pe: The Mouth

Technical Data: The seventeenth letter of the Hebrew alphabet is *pe*, and 343 words in the Hebrew Bible start with *pe*. Of these, 94 are proper names and places, and 249 are regular words. The Greek equivalent of *pe* is *pi*, and our English letter is "p."

Jewish Definitions: Jewish writers state that *pe* is the symbol of speech as well as silence. One writer stated, "*Pe* or mouth makes man as a human being able to fulfill the ultimate purpose of creation: to sing the praises of the Almighty and to speak out His word."

Christian Definitions: Consulting eight sources, all read "mouth." Dr. James Strong also adds, "...blowing with the mouth, literally or figuratively. Particularly speech, sound, sentence and words."

Devotional Comments

Pe is the seventeenth Hebrew letter, and it represents a mouth. There are more than 400 references to the mouth in scripture. In addition, there are another 10,330 references to speech in such words as "say," "speak," "word," and so forth. Evidently the mouth is of vital importance, both in the Bible and in our everyday life.

The ability to speak is one of the joys of human life. What a great difference exists between humans and animals! The human was created with the God-given ability to speak and to communicate with words.

Although animals make certain sounds to express their various responses, they will never have the capacity to learn to communicate by speaking words. Speech is one of the essential vehicles of the Creator, and He designed Adam and Eve with the same capacity.

Although the power of speech is a lofty privilege, it seems that the mouth does not enjoy a good reputation. This is because six millennia of sin have so eroded, warped, and polluted human language and speech that communication is only a shadow of what it should be.

We all have encountered the kind of mouth that is, in reality, a weapon. (Its tongue is a sword, its teeth like daggers, and its lips are the opening to an awful pit. Need we continue?) But in spite of its gross misuse, the mouth can be one of the noblest of our faculties, as we see from the following scriptures.

> **The words of a man's mouth are as deep waters, and the wellspring of wisdom as a flowing brook.**
>
> **Proverbs 18:4**

> **The tongue of the righteous is as choice silver.**
>
> **Proverbs 10:20**

> **Every man shall kiss his lips that giveth a right answer.**
>
> **Proverbs 24:26**

> **The lips of the righteous feed many....**
>
> **Proverbs 10:21**

There is a vital connection between one's heart and one's mouth. Jesus said, "Out of the overflow of the heart the mouth speaks" (Matthew 12:34). If a person has evil in his heart, he has, as a consequence, a problem mouth: "A fool's mouth is his destruction, and his lips are the snare of his soul" (Proverbs 18:7).

What makes God's words so conspicuously different from ours is that His nature is perfectly righteous; His heart is absolutely pure; and, therefore, His words are clear, concise, pure, honest, straightforward, and totally devoid of any trickery, sarcasm, dishonesty, or unfairness: "The words of the Lord are pure words: as silver tried in a furnace of earth, purified seven times" (Psalm 12:6).

This shows that God's words are unlike those of everyone else. His Word is mighty, unchanging, and perfect. It is also *final*. Thus, the powerful Hebrew phrase *kiy piy Adonai diber* ("for the mouth of the Lord has spoken") is intended to convey *absolute certainty*. This phrase occurs several times in the Prophets. No one can reverse what God has proclaimed, because His Word is forever established in heaven (Psalm 119:89).

When God placed words in a prophet's mouth, that prophet's mouth became akin to God's mouth. For example, Jeremiah said, "Then the Lord put forth His hand, and touched my mouth. And the Lord said to me, Behold, I have put my words in your mouth" (Jeremiah 1:9).

Jeremiah 15:19 is similar: "If you take forth the precious from the vile, you shall be as my mouth." Also, Moses gave commandments exactly as he received them from the Lord; he enjoyed a very personal access to the counsel of the Lord. The scripture records that God spoke with him "mouth to mouth" in a clear manner (Numbers 12:8).

But the most harmonization between the mouth of God and that of any man was realized through the Prophet spoken of in Deuteronomy 18:15,18,19. The Lord said to Moses, "I will raise up for them a Prophet like you from among their brothers: I will put my words in his mouth, and he will tell them everything I command him. If any one does not listen to my words that the Prophet speaks in my name, I myself will call him to account."

How do we know that this specific Prophet was Jesus? First, because Jesus fulfilled the requirements of being "like Moses." The parallels in their lives are beyond coincidence or human contrivance!

Both Moses and Jesus were born at a time when the children of Israel were oppressed by hostile foreign governments. Both Moses and Jesus were placed in great danger when bloodthirsty tyrants ordered that all Jewish male infants should be killed. Pharaoh gave this decree when Moses was born, and Herod gave similar orders when Jesus was less than two years of age.

Both Moses and Jesus were spared from death by the protective actions taken by their faithful, God-fearing parents. Both Moses and Jesus in early childhood found nourishment and safety in Egypt. Both looked with compassion on the condition of their Hebrew brethren.

Both were destined by God to be the deliverer of the nation of Israel. Both were immediately scorned and ridiculed when they first came to the aid of their brothers. Both were initially rejected and misunderstood by the people whom God sent them to deliver.

Both were willing to offer their lives that Israel should be forgiven and reconciled to God! (Compare Exodus 32:30-34 with John 11:49-52, Acts 3:25,26, and Second Corinthians 5:18,19.) Both are known as the greatest of the intercessors for God's people. And there is so much more that makes Moses and Jesus similar.

What confirms the prophecy in Deuteronomy 18 to the fullest, however, is the fulfillment of God's pledge that if anyone failed to heed the Lord's words through this Prophet, He Himself would require the people to account for their refusal to listen.

Failing to heed Moses and Joshua cost the Exodus generation 40 years in the wilderness. Failing to heed Jeremiah cost the inhabitants of Judah the loss of the first Temple and 70 years of captivity in Babylon!

Failing to heed Jesus, the Prophet foretold in Deuteronomy 18, cost the inhabitants of Judea the loss of the Temple, Jerusalem, and nationhood, and resulted in more than 1,800 years of exile!

The rejection of the Greater Prophet brought a greater delaying of God's promised blessings than did the rejection of Moses and Jeremiah combined and multiplied many times over!

No one in history lived a life with more similarities to Moses than did Jesus; nor has God required an account for the rejection of any prophet to the degree or duration that He has in regard to Jesus.

Furthermore, God told Moses that this Prophet would tell the people everything that God had instructed Him to speak. Jesus showed that He was the Prophet in question when He said:

> **I have not spoken of myself; but the Father who sent me has given me a commandment, what I should say and what I should speak.**
>
> **I know that His commandment is everlasting life. So whatever I say is just what the Father has told me to say.**
>
> **John 12:49,50**

Because Jesus spoke God's words faithfully, His hearers were moved by what He had to say. What must it have been like to listen to His words? We have some picture of the effect of His speech in John 7:45,46. Certain officers who had been sent to apprehend Jesus reported back to the chief priests empty-handed.

"Why haven't you brought him?" the chief priests demanded.

The officers gave this meaningful reply: "No man ever *spoke* like this man!"

Most of us are familiar with what Jesus said about the power of His words: His words will judge mankind at the last day; His voice will awaken the dead from all past generations; His words will never pass away, although heaven and Earth change.

But there is something to be noted beyond the power of the words of His mouth (which is itself beyond comprehension). It is the *character* of His mouth that distinguished Him from others.

The scripture says it best in First Peter 2:22,23. The first sentence of this quotation is repeated from Isaiah 53:9:

He committed no sin, and no deceit was found in his mouth. When he was insulted, he did not retaliate. When he suffered, he made no threats. Instead, he entrusted himself to Him who judges righteously.

This beautiful tribute from one of Jesus' closest disciples, Simon Peter, declares that Jesus' speech was absolutely without deceit, guile, or deception. It was a way of life for Jesus to speak without guile.

Not only that, but when He was under unbearable pressure, insults, and physical suffering, He *never* misused His mouth, nor did He lash out with harsh words. He was the *Lamb*; and as a lamb is dumb before her shearers, He did not open His mouth.

You are challenged to identify any person in history who could fulfill all the minute details of Isaiah 53 and who responded before His accusers in the manner that verse 7 specifies. Only One has done so.

This letter *pe* represents the mouth — and hence the words of our great Shepherd.

The words of Jesus hold the material universe in place and have repeatedly proved capable of supporting our very lives.

(Pronounced TZAH-DEE)

Chapter 18
Tzaddi: A Fishhook

Technical Data: Tzaddi is the eighteenth letter of the Hebrew alphabet, and 265 words in the Hebrew Bible start with *tzaddi*. Of these, 72 are proper names and places, and 193 are regular words. It is not easy to determine the Greek equivalent; one writer said *sigma*.

Jewish Definitions: Etz Yosef states, "*Tzaddi* is a symbol of righteousness and humility. The bent letter *tzaddi* stands for the righteous bent in humility. The final *tzaddi* is tall showing that the righteous who is bent in humility in this world will at last be tall and erect in the world to come."

Christian Definitions: While most authors quoted "fishhook" as the definition of *tzaddi, Davies-Mitchell Lexicon* states "to catch." Hastings says it is "a javelin" or "a hook." *International Standard* says, "*Tzaddi* means trap, hook, noose, and steps." Both MacMillan and Montgomerie define *tzaddi* as "surrender." The fishhook theme is evident in all the definitions. Sidon the Bible city (Tyre and Sidon) is from this Hebrew letter and literally means "a place for catching fish or fishery."

Devotional Comments

The eighteenth letter, *tzaddi*, signifies a fishhook. As we mentioned in the chapter on letter *nun*, fishing is a very ancient occupation. A further proof of this is furnished by the letter *tzaddi:* If Hebrew is a most ancient tongue, and if one of its letters represents a fishhook, then evidently people have been fishing for quite some time.

The root word from which *tzaddi* comes is *tsayid*, which means "the catching, hunting, or chasing of food," such as fish or game. *Tsayid* comes from the verb *tsuwd*, which means "to lie in wait, to catch an animal (or even a person), to chase, hunt, and take." It is easy to see that the early concepts of hunting and fishing were closely linked linguistically.

There are two seldom-mentioned prophecies in scripture which employ the metaphor of fishhooks or fishing and which speak of the forces which would lead Israel into and then out of exile. (For those who might not know, the biblical and secular term for the dispersion of the Jewish people among the nations is *Diaspora*.)

In Amos 4:2, the Lord declares that His people are about to be drawn away by fishhooks into captivity among the various nations: "The Lord God has sworn by His holiness that the days shall come upon you that He will take you away with *hooks* and your posterity with *fishhooks.*"

Here the picture is one of fishhooks pulling the people in an irresistible manner and dragging them to the respective nations of their captivity. A fish being dragged out of its native waters by means of hook and line is traveling in a direction in which it has no desire to go. Similarly, the forces which brought Israel into captivity were compelling forces.

But Jeremiah 16:16 shows that it is also compelling forces (fishers and hunters) who bring Israel back from the *Diaspora*. The preceding verse speaks of the time when God would bring up "the sons of Israel from the land of the north and from all lands where He had driven them" (verse 15). The verse concludes, "and I will bring them again into the land that I gave to their fathers."

The next sentence, verse 16, shows how this regathering will occur: "Behold, I will send for many *fishermen*, says the Lord, and they shall fish for them; and after this I will send for many *hunters*, and they will hunt them from every mountain, and from every hill, and out of the clefts of the rocks."

Anyone living in this century can see that God has regathered Israel from all countries. (Unless a person is completely comatose, this regathering has not escaped his or her notice!)

Who were the fishermen and who were the hunters? Who is it that has caused the attention of the whole world to be focused on the household of Jacob — a people so comparatively few in number that they account for much less than one half of one percent of the world's population?

The fishermen were the early Zionists who aroused much interest in the return to the land of Israel. When the fishermen had captured as many pioneers as they could, the hunters arrived on the scene in the 1930s.

The hunters have been all the violent anti-Semitic forces worldwide which have made it their business to hunt down and harass the Jewish people. The violent spirit behind this activity has never been ashamed of the recent and continuing deeds of barbarism and murder. On the contrary, this evil force is spreading violence and hatred against the people of the Book in more countries than ever before!

This relentless and hateful spirit serves two purposes. First, it has compelled many people to return to Israel. Second, when fully developed, it will draw all nations into an attack against Israel, at which time God personally will destroy all those nations which are attempting to annihilate His chosen nation. (See Zephaniah 3:8,9 and Zechariah 12:3,9.)

This intervention on God's part will itself serve two major purposes. First and most important, it will forever exalt the God of Israel as the Sovereign God of creation in the eyes of all the survivors from those nations which went against Jerusalem. Second, it will once and for all demonstrate to the world that the people of Israel are chosen of God.

Those who hate Israel hate God as well. Those who persecute Israel seek their own destruction. This is an inescapable truth of scripture and an irrefutable fact of history which offers no other explanation but a divine one.

In the same vein as God's drawing all nations to this rendezvous in Jerusalem, we find the prophecy of the Prince of Rosh in Ezekiel 38 and 39. There we read how God will draw the evil prince of the North to attack Israel. The Lord pledges to completely smash this northern empire and to rescue His people.

How does God induce one of the world's superpowers to come "out of the north parts" to attempt to overtake little Israel? It is *with hooks*, as we find in Ezekiel 38:4. God says, "I will put *hooks* in your jaws, and I will bring you forth and all your army...."

This may be a reference to the way that crocodiles were snared in ancient times; particularly in Egypt. A strong iron hook was baited and attached to ropes. When the crocodile lunged for the bait, the hook pierced his jaw, and the hunters dragged the thrashing monster out by pulling in the ropes.

What the world perceives to be a frightening and dangerous empire God sees as merely a repulsive crocodile about to be baited, hooked, and then dragged to its doom! The picture is actually humorous when we think about it.

There are many references to fishing in the New Testament. These references carry a very positive connotation. We read that Jesus fished. He chose fishermen for disciples. When they were unsuccessful on one occasion, He told them what to do in order to get a big haul of fish.

When Jesus selected His disciples, He told them that He would cause them to fish for men. (See Matthew 4:19.) By the wisdom of God, their natural talents for scouting out fish and gathering them in would be developed into a talent for gathering people!

Jesus gave a particular parable which uses the example of fishing to illustrate the coming harvest of people:

> The kingdom of heaven is like a net that was let down
> into the lake and caught all kinds of fish.
>
> When it was full, the fishermen pulled it up on the shore.
> Then they sat down and collected the good fish in baskets,
> but threw the bad away.
>
> This is how it will be at the end of the age.
>
> **Matthew 13:47-49** *NIV*

It would be appropriate to mention that much of the fishing done by the disciples involved the use of nets rather than hooks. Both the netting and the hooking of fish can come under the definition of *tsayid*, from which the letter *tzaddi* comes.

It is noteworthy that Jesus instructed Peter to cast out a "hook" in order to catch the fish which contained the tax money (Matthew 17:27). So we observe that both methods of taking fish — hooking and netting — existed at the same time, just as they both do now.

Jesus was eminently qualified to teach His disciples how to fish for people, because He had the wonderful ability to draw people to Himself. His was a loving, warm, and magnetic personality that naturally appealed to everything good within humanity. (See John 1:16; 3:21.)

The scriptures state that He ministered only to the people of Israel, and how popular He was with His fellow Jews may be shown from the following verses. In Luke 19:47,48, we find that the chief priests were unable to stop Him from teaching daily at the Temple, because *"all* the people were very attentive to hear Him."

We find in Mark 3:10 that Jesus healed so many people that sick persons crowded around Him and "pressed upon him to touch him." (See also Luke 8:45.) On another occasion, as He was discoursing in the Temple, we read that "the common people heard him gladly" (Mark 12:37).

Finally, in John 12:17-19 we see that the people who were eyewitnesses when Jesus raised Lazarus from the dead caused Jesus' fame to increase; the effect was that more and more people went out to meet with Jesus.

This caused the religious leaders to feel that all their efforts to control the people and to restrict Jesus had failed. "The Pharisees said to one another, 'See, this is getting us nowhere. Look how the *whole world* has gone after him!'" With the notable exception of most of the religious leaders who were jealous of Jesus' success with the people, those who saw and heard Jesus were greatly drawn to Him.

Speaking of the Messiah, Genesis 49:10 says, "unto Him shall the gathering of the people be." The actual title *Shiloh* in verse 10 has been translated "Peacebringer," but probably a more accurate translation of *Shiloh* would be "He to whom it belongs"; that is, he to whom the scepter of the kingdom belongs.

Therefore, this scripture may be understood to say, "The scepter shall not depart from Judah, nor a lawgiver from among his descendants, until He comes to whom the scepter belongs, and unto *Him* shall the gathering of the peoples be." Note that the Hebrew wording of Genesis 49:10 says "peoples"; this is to say that entire nations, tribes, and races will gather adoringly around the Lord Jesus!

There is a wonderful process of being drawn to Jesus which multitudes of persons from every nation have experienced for 20 centuries. Simeon and Anna in the Temple and the stargazers from the East were among the first who were drawn to Him, and the divinely ordered attraction has not ceased to this day, nor will it ever cease.

Jesus said, "No one can come to me unless the Father who sent me draws him, and I will raise him up at the last day. It is written in the Prophets, 'They will all be taught by God.' Everyone who listens to the Father and learns from him comes to me" (John 6:44,45 *NIV*).

Tzaddi is that fishhook that works best in drawing human beings to the Savior of the whole world.

(Pronounced KOHF)

Chapter 19
Qoph: Back of the Head

Technical Data: Qoph is the nineteenth letter of the Hebrew alphabet, and 308 words in the Hebrew Bible start with *qoph.* Of these, 60 are proper names and places, and 248 are regular words. There is no Greek equivalent to *qoph.* Our English letter is "q."

Jewish Definitions: One Jewish source, *Shabbos,* states, "The letter *qoph* alludes to God's holiness." Another writer said, "*Qoph* is a symbol of holiness and growth cycles."

Christian Definitions: "Back of the head." *Davies-Mitchell Lexicon* reads, "the nape." Gesenius likens it to the hole of an ax for securing the ax head to the handle. *Hastings Bible Dictionary* calls it "a knot." *International Standard* states, "a cage, an outline of the head and a helmet."

There is a *qoph* of foreign origin meaning "ape" or "monkey." (See Strong's number 6971 — Old Testament.) Also, the *Wycliffe Bible Encyclopedia,* defining *qoph,* says "monkey," but adds a question mark, as though they are not sure.

Both MacMillan and Montgomerie, who have written books on the Hebrew alphabet, define *qoph* as "the hole of an ax head." MacMillan spiritualizes *qoph,* saying that it is "power lost and regained."

Devotional Comments

The nineteenth Hebrew letter is *qoph.* As was stated in the word study, there are several possible meanings for *qoph.* One of our most accurate reference encyclopedias declines to define *qoph* at all! *Qoph* ia a unique letter for this reason, and it is also remarkable for its visual similarity to its cognate letter, the letter "q," in our Roman alphabet.

When we consider the possible definitions of *qoph* ("nape of the neck, back of head, neck, helmet, hole of ax head"), we wonder what common ground exists among these meanings. The most apparent similarity in these meanings is that each has something to do with the head at its juncture with the neck.

A neck (whether of an implement or the anatomical one) is of crucial importance, being by design a focal point of stress. The neck of an ax or a hammer must be made of especially hard wood in order to sustain the heavy blows for which the implement is designed.

The neck fits through the metal hole, which lends cushioning and support and is strategically designed to maximize the tool's efficiency. In a similar sense, a helmet on a person's head cushions the head, lends support, and can protect against undue neck stress.

When an ax, maul, or hammer breaks, the location of the fracture is invariably the neck. This is why we find more replacement handles than ax heads or maul heads in hardware stores. It is proof that designers of such implements expect there will be occasions when the tools will break at the neck.

We can see how vulnerable the human neck is by considering that in traffic accidents, even when seat restraints have prevented the most critical injuries, neck injuries are quite common.

Fracturing is not the only danger to the neck of an ax. If the wedges are not secure enough, or if there is a wearing down of the wooden piece that fits through the metal hole, the ax head may slip off entirely. This happens frequently. It even happened to one poor ax swinger in Bible times. The young man was more upset than he would normally have been, because the ax was borrowed. This account is found in Second Kings 6:5-7.

So far, we have stated that the neck is easily broken, prone to fracture and other problems, and is the location that receives the greatest strain. All this is merely to show how vital the neck is.

A properly built tool, made of the hardest wood and carefully fitted, if properly used should be able to withstand any strain not greater than that for which it was designed.

As we examine the relationship of a person's neck to his head, some things are immediately apparent. First, while the head contains all the most important senses (the head being the house of the brain, eyes, ears, taste, and smell and being the terminus of all touch perception; and the mind itself being the control center for the whole body), the neck is nonetheless of great importance.

Through the nerves inside the neck pass all incoming reports from other parts of the body; and, more important, through it pass all the brain's commands to direct all the rest of the body — arms, legs, hands, feet, and so on.

The body would not be able to function without directions from the brain, but neither would the brain be able to direct the body members to walk, write, move, and function if it had no connection to these other body members. Of course, that connection is through the spinal column, which first passes through the neck.

It is common knowledge that when people have severe neck injuries, they often lose feeling in other parts of the body. Sometimes they lose the ability to use their body entirely, either from the waist down or from the neck down.

Second, the neck is the pedestal upon which the head is supposed to rest. It not only supports the head; it also allows the head to turn to either side or tilt up and down.

Even wicked King Joram, in a fit of rage over the prophet Elisha, confessed in a backwards sort of way that the head is normally supposed to rest atop the body. Joram cried, "May God deal with me, be it ever so severely, if the head of Elisha son of Shaphat shall stand on his shoulders today!" (2 Kings 6:31). The king, of course, failed to kill Elisha, whose head continued to rest majestically upon his body for the duration of his ministry.

As we have been commenting on *qoph,* we have brought out the concept of an ax head, neck, and handle along with its corresponding physiological structure — head, neck, and body. We have stressed that the *qoph,* the point of juncture of the head and body, is one of the most delicate and vital connections in the body.

This is where the Lord comes into the picture. Many scriptures declare that the Lord Jesus is the "Head," and those who belong to Him are His "Body." (We will be referring to these verses in the following chapter.)

This illustration of head and body clearly proves that Jesus by His thoughts, wishes, and counsels, which are revealed in the scriptures, should direct and coordinate harmoniously the motions of His Body in the same way impulses coming from one's head direct the rest of his body, be it for running, dancing, working, or any of a hundred other skillful activities!

Ephesians 4:15,16 says it beautifully: "Speaking the truth in love, we will in all things grow up unto Him who is the Head, that is, the Messiah. From Him the whole body, *joined and held together* by every supporting ligament, grows and builds itself up in love, as each part does its work."

Thus, the head adroitly guides and directs the entire body. But this presupposes that the head and the body are joined together, and the body is able to receive impulses from the head. If the Body is dislocated from its Head, the Lord's will is no more expressed through His Body than a quadriplegic can express his will through his body! The neck is this all-important point of juncture, and it speaks to us of our great responsibility to be joined and submitted to the Lord.

Jesus said, "The foxes have holes, and the birds of the air have nests; but the Son of man has no place to lay his head" (Matthew 8:20). While He had no house of His own, He did live with Peter's family, so He must have had some place to rest at least part of the time.

Is Jesus saying more than the obvious, "I do not have a home"? Why did He say that He had no place to lay His head? Is it because He, the great Head of the Body of believers, had not found a company of righteous people to whom He could be fitly joined and through whom He could express His holy and sinless nature? Was He not declaring that He would not rest until He had provided the way for this great joining to be accomplished?

We know from the scriptures that the Father is preparing a Bride for Jesus. When She (that is to say, those who are to be given to Him) is complete, He will enter into His reign, and all the Earth will enter into the Sabbath rest of God.

Qoph is the place of joining for the ax head and its handle, for the head and the body — and for Jesus and the Redeemed!

(Pronounced REYSH)

Chapter 20
Resh: The Head — First in Rank and Order

Technical Data: Resh is the twentieth letter of the Hebrew alphabet, 379 words in the Hebrew Bible start with *resh*. Of these, 76 are proper names and places, and 303 are regular words. The Greek equivalent is *rho*. Our English letter is "r."

Jewish Definitions: The *Midrash Hagadol* says of *resh*, "This is the Holy One, blessed is he. He is the head of the entire world and he is the end of the entire world." Rabbi Akiva identifies *resh* as *rosh*, the head or beginning. This is a reference to God.

Christian Definitions: Ten sources consulted all concur that *resh* is the head in the sense of first in place, time, rank, etc. It applies to the physical head as well as the beginning, the chief, the ruler (for example, heads of state).

Devotional Comments

Letter 20 is *resh*, which represents "a head." *Resh* and its companion forms *rosh, rishon,* and *resheet* have a very wide range of applications. Included in these words are the following meanings: "one's physical head, head of state, ruler, com-

115

mander, head of tribe, head of a race, patriarch, first father, first in line, firstfruits, chief, head of the corner (or as we say, cornerstone), top of a mountain, primary, principal, foremost, preeminent, and beginning."

It is impossible to miss the sense of primary conveyed by the words *resh* and *rosh*. In fact, the first word in the Bible — *beresheet*, translated "in the beginning" — is literally "at the *first*," and comes from the word *resh*.

In addition to carrying such important meanings, *resh* and its other forms mentioned above are notable for their frequent occurrence in scripture, appearing more than 800 times.

Most of the preceding definitions appear in scripture as titles of our Lord Jesus. We will examine 12 biblical titles of Jesus the Messiah which have to do with *resh* and *rosh*. These scriptures leave no doubt as to the foremost position of the Anointed One!

Jesus is called *"the chief cornerstone"* in Ephesians 2:20 and again in First Peter 2:6: "Behold I lay in Zion a chief corner stone, chosen, precious: and he that believes on Him shall not be ashamed."

The beautiful Hebrew phrase *rosh pinah* — *"the head of the corner"* — is used in Psalm 118:22: "The stone which the builders rejected is come to be the head of the corner." (See also Luke 20:17; Acts 4:11; and First Peter 2:7.)

In Colossians 1:18; 2:19, Jesus is called *"the head of the body."* He is called *"the head of the church"* in Ephesians 5:23. (See also Ephesians 1:22.) Another title of Jesus is *"the first-fruits"* (1 Corinthians 15:20). This has to do with His being the first one to receive a resurrected and glorified body.

In Colossians 1:18, He is called *"the firstborn from the dead"*: "And he is the head of the body, the church: who is the beginning, the firstborn from the dead; that in all things He might have the preeminence." In this verse, there are four words related to the idea of *resh*: head, beginning, firstborn, and preeminence.

He is called *"the firstbegotten"* in Hebrews 1:6 and *"the firstborn"* in Romans 8:29 and Hebrews 12:23. In Luke 2:7, He is called the *"firstborn son."*

Jesus is known as *"the captain of our salvation"* (Hebrews 2:10). He is also *"the FIRST and the last"* (Revelation 1:17). The final title which we will note in this section is *"ruler."* Micah 5:2 says that out of little Bethlehem shall come forth "He that is to be ruler in Israel."

When the angel announced to the mother of Jesus the glad news that she was to bear the Messiah, there was no doubt that this child was destined to be Israel's ruler:

He shall be great, and shall be called the Son of the Highest: and the Lord God shall give unto him the throne of his father David:

And he shall reign over the house of Jacob for ever; and of his kingdom there shall be no end"

Luke 1:32,33

All other rulers' kingdoms have eventually perished in human history, but *Jesus our Messiah will reign forever!* The kings of history have often struggled violently to gain power, and then ruthlessly employed violence, lying, brute force, and every means available to hold on to power for their brief reign.

Some have destroyed everyone who disagreed with them and expended all their energies in their mad pursuit of power — and for what? For one year, 10 years, or even 20 years of glory? How foolish! Contrast them with Jesus, who first laid down His very life for His citizens, and then by the Lord God's decree will rule forever and forever!

As we have seen from the preceding 12 titles of Jesus the chief, captain, ruler, head, and first of all, the Bible ascribes a place to Him of preeminence in all things. He is the first one, the head, and the leader, and His is the primary position: "He is before all things, and by him all things consist" (Colossians 1:17).

God spoke this promise to David concerning his great descendant Jesus: "I will make him my *firstborn,* higher than the kings of the earth" (Psalm 89:27). Consistent with such a great position is His great name: "God has given him a name above every other name, that at the name of Jesus every knee should bow...and every tongue confess that Jesus the Messiah is Lord, to the glory of God the Father" (Philippians 2:9-11).

Resh is the preeminent firstborn exalted King, the Head of God's new creation — Jesus the Lord!

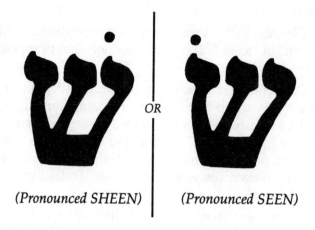

(*Pronounced SHEEN*) | (*Pronounced SEEN*)

Chapter 21
Shin or *Sin:* Tooth

Technical Data: Shin or *sin* is the twenty-first letter of the Hebrew alphabet. The *shin-sin* series has 793 words. Of these, 219 are proper names and places, and 574 are regular words. The Greek equivalent is *sigma.* Our English letters are "sh" for *shin* and "s" for *sin.*

Shin and *sin* are look-alike letters. The pronunciation is determined by a dot placed above the crown. If the dot is placed above the crown on the left, the letter is *sin.* If the dot is placed above the crown on the right, the letter is *shin.* The consonants s-l-m could spell either *salem* or *shalom,* depending on how the "s" letter is marked.

Jewish Definitions: One Jewish writer likens *shin* and *sin* to assimilating the Word of God by chewing, swallowing, and digesting the truth of God as written in the Book of the Lord. The shape of the *shin* resembles a molar, which crushes food with its three sharply edged cusps.

As the tooth grinds the food to make it digestible for the body, so shall teaching *(shanan)* transmit the Word of

119

God in such a well-analyzed manner that it can be absorbed by the mind.

Christian Definitions: Ten writers consulted record *shin* as "tooth" or "teeth." The word does not seem to appear anywhere in the Bible.

One writer consulted did quote Isaiah 41:15, "I will make of you a new sharp threshing instrument having teeth and you shall thresh the mountains and make them small and make the hills as chaff." This writer says we are to have a keen edge, possess the (competitive) edge, and have wisdom teeth. However, the word for "teeth" in that passage is *piphiyah*, not *shin*.

There is a reference to the grinding action of teeth slowing down in old age found in Ecclesiastes 12:3,4. But the word is *tachanah*, not *shin*.

The Song of Solomon has several references to teeth (4:2; 6:6). In poetic language, the bridegroom praises the beautiful teeth of the bride and likens them to a flock of sheep. The word he uses is *shen* (pronounced "shane"). This word is closely related to our words *shin* and *sin*.

Devotional Comments

The twenty-first Hebrew letter, *shin* or *sin*, represents a tooth. Note: This letter *shin* or *sin* counts as only one letter of the alphabet. As can be seen from an illustration of the letters, the shape is the same for *shin* and *sin*; only the point changes, and that determines if the letter represents a "sh" or a "s" sound.

So there are two Hebrew letters which represent the sound "s" — *samech* and *sin*. Ordinarily, the words which start with the letter *samech* are consistently spelled with a *samech* rather than a *sin*, and vice versa. This means that the spelling of words beginning with "s" must be memorized.

However, there is sometimes a certain amount of substitution of *sin* for *samech*, or of *samech* for *sin*. We might compare this to the way that "v" and "f" are sometimes interchanged in English, as in the words "believe" and "belief," or, better yet, the way "z" and "s" are interchanged in many words, such as "apologize" and "apologise." As we bear all this in mind, we will discover something fascinating about a famous biblical site whose name is derived from the word for "tooth."

The word "tooth" in Hebrew is *shen*, from which we get our letter *shin*. *Shen* means "tooth, sharp, crag, cliff, ivory, and forefront." The first set of meanings we will examine concerns "sharp" and "craggy." Mountain ranges which have sharp, craggy, tooth-like peaks often bear the name "Sierra," such as the Sierra Nevada, Sierra Madre, and so forth. In Spanish, the word *sierra* literally means "the teeth of a saw" or "sawtooth." From a distance, the outline of the sharp peaks resembles the teeth of a saw blade. This is how mountain ranges have acquired their existing names in the English- and Spanish-speaking worlds; the Sawtooth Mountains would be an example from the English language.

Is there a similar case in Hebrew? Yes there is — and it involves the well-known and important biblical mountain called *Sinai*. People have argued over the meaning of *Sinai* for generations. It is doubtful that this chapter will end all the disputing. Nevertheless, the opinion that seems to be the most sound is that *Sinai* and the related word "wilderness of *Sin*" come from *sin* and *shin* and therefore mean "sharp, craggy, tooth-like, thorn-like" as a description of the rocky and rugged spires of the Sinai range.

Sinai is spelled with a *samech* and not a *sin*, but, as we can prove through biblical examples, the substitution of the one letter for the other is not too uncommon.

One rabbinic interpretation develops the association of *sinai* with "teeth." It seems that one of the alternate names of Mount Sinai — *Har Bashan* — is interpreted by the rabbis to mean "the mountain with the teeth," which, as they understand, suggests that "mankind through the virtue of this mountain obtains its sustenance." The idea is that the teeth are a vital necessity for chewing one's nourishment.

The next set of meanings in the word *shen* has to do with hardness. We find that *shen* is translated both by the words "teeth" and "ivory." It is a fact that the hardest substance in the human body is the enamel of the teeth. This substance is so hard that its friction with steel will generate sparks! This represents firmness.

The teeth are also firmly embedded by means of roots. One might wonder which is easier: to pull up a tree by its roots or to pull out a tooth by its roots. Teeth convey the idea of firmness, inflexibility, permanence, and durability.

Strength is the factor that binds all these concepts together. Isaiah 41:14,15 illustrates this idea. Israel felt as defenseless as a worm, but God promised to provide them with teeth strong enough to crush mountains!

> **Do not be afraid, O worm Jacob, O little Israel, for I myself will help you, declares the Lord your Redeemer, the Holy One of Israel.**

> **Behold I will make you into a threshing instrument, new and sharp, with many teeth. You will thresh the mountains and crush them, and reduce the hills to chaff.**

What a picture of strength!

We cannot forget that teeth are also a picture of beauty. There is something magnificent about perfect teeth, and there is something attractive about a friendly smile that reveals the teeth in all their beauty.

In the Song of Songs we read the compliments exchanged between the Shulamite girl and her beloved. One verse (6:6) extols the beauty of her teeth: "Your teeth are like a flock of sheep coming up from the washing. Each has its twin, not one of them is alone."

What do firm, sharp, perfect teeth have to do with anything *spiritual?* First, let us note that the biblical prophets were given messages with "teeth" to them. In their day, as in ours, what was needed was not another weak voice proclaiming, in the words of the old Latin phrase, "The voice of the people is the voice of God."

What was required was a factual, truthful representation of the state of affairs and the rightful means of bringing correction. It did not matter that the prophets' strong words were not popular. *What mattered is that they were true!*

The religious world may be symbolized by its legions of pulpits in which there is a sad lack of any preaching of a message with "teeth" — any words which can correctly pierce and identify the real cause of the world's anguish: the sinful condition of humanity.

The prophets spoke firmly with God-given authority, and so did Jesus:

> **They went into Capernaum, and on the Sabbath day He entered into the synagogue, and taught.**
>
> **And they were astonished at His doctrine: for He taught them as one that had authority, and not as the scribes.**
>
> **Mark 1:21,22**

Contrasted with Jesus are evil men whose teeth "bite and devour." Unlike them, *Jesus used His mouth to speak only truth, correction, and healing.*

As He was dying, the onlookers tried to provoke and taunt Him with ridicule, and the other men crucified with Him "cast the same taunts in His teeth" (Matthew 27:44). But He never retaliated. He simply spoke forgiveness to the one dying criminal who asked for His help (Luke 23:42,43).

Through *shin* we see that *Messiah's teeth are righteous, firm, and strong to speak truth.*

Isaiah 42:4 says, "He shall not fail nor be discouraged, till He has set judgment in the earth: and the islands will wait and hope for His law."

This means that the ends of the Earth will eagerly wait for pronouncements from King Jesus' mouth — laws that will end every dispute and set justice in the Earth! His teeth, words, and decrees are absolutely perfect. *Shin* represents His perfect teeth.

(Pronounced TAHV)

Chapter 22
Tav: The Cross-Shaped Mark or Sign

Technical Data: The Hebrew alphabet begins with *aleph*, a sacrificial animal (one used in the shedding of blood), and ends with *tav*, the mark of the cross.

Tav is the twenty-second letter of the Hebrew alphabet, and 302 words in the Hebrew Bible start with *tav.* Of these, 75 are proper names, and 227 are regular words. The Greek equivalent is *tau.* Our English letter is "t," which has retained its cross shape. (In ancient Hebrew and in Aramaic, *tav* represented, under certain circumstances, a "th" sound.)

Jewish Definitions: The *Midrash Hagadol* states, "The very first sign mentioned in scripture (Genesis 4:15) was placed by God Himself who inscribed a single letter of the alphabet on Cain's forehead. The sign was made in [the] form of a *tav.*"

Another writer points out that "in Ezekiel 9 a *tav* was put on the foreheads of the righteous ones destined for life in the world to come. *Tav* is the most fitting letter to symbolize man's final destination."

Christian Definitions: Davies-Mitchell Lexicon defines *tav* as "the sign of the cross"; most other writers consulted use the word "cross" or "mark." Hastings' Dictionary adds "a sign for marking animals." Gesenius states "a sign in the form of a cross." John Montgomerie declares "*tav* is a sign or a mark put on [something]."

An example of *tav* is found in Ezekiel 9:4: "Go through the midst of the city...and set a mark [*tav*] upon the foreheads of the men that sigh and cry for all the abominations that be done in the midst thereof." Verses 5 and 6: "smite and slay...but come not near any man upon whom is the mark [*tav*]; and begin at my sanctuary."

Having the mark of the cross qualified them for being spared in the judgment!

Devotional Comments

The twenty-second letter of the Hebrew alphabet, *tav*, is the final letter. It represents "a mark, signature, brand, or sign." From the earliest centuries in which we have archaeological examples of Hebrew script — which is about 2,900 years ago — every example of Hebrew lettering from scrolls, inscriptions, coins, and stone has the letter *tav* as a cross shape of some type.

The first case of the "modern" *tav* in which there is no intersection of lines occurred in Palmyra in the third century A.D. (See *Jewish Encyclopedia*, Volume 1, pages 449-453.)

Soon all Hebrew scripts followed suit and dropped the cross-shaped *tav*. Perhaps this indicated that its ancient form, which had been in use from at least Solomon's time through the beginning of the decline of Rome, was *no longer acceptable.*

The word *tav* means "mark." Since earliest times, people have put a mark on their own possessions; especially in the case of livestock. Marking or branding one's animals was a real necessity, since the flocks of several shepherds were often required to feed together or travel together.

Because of all the intermingling and "socializing" that would naturally occur among the flocks, there was a need for some means whereby a shepherd could find his own sheep or cattle and with total certainty say, "These are mine!" The simplest means of identification is to put a mark on the animals which will link them to their owner.

Many scriptures, such as Ezekiel 34:31, declare that God's people are His flock, the sheep of His pasture: "You my sheep, the sheep of my pasture, are people, and I am your God, declares the Sovereign Lord." (See also Psalm 100:3; Isaiah 40:11; Jeremiah 23:3; 31:10; Ezekiel 34:2-30; 36:38; Zechariah 10:3.)

If the Lord's flock consists of people, are there any marks which identify them as His own? Yes, indeed there are. In the Bible we find a good number of distinguishing marks of God's people, and we shall begin to look at some of these marks which God has chosen to employ.

The first mark of God's people is circumcision (Genesis 17:11), which God gave as a "token of the covenant" between Himself and Abraham. (We will find that our letter *tav* is consistently linked to the concept of covenant as we continue.)

The mark of circumcision was given in order to identify the sons of God's covenant with Abraham and to remind his descendants of their binding agreement to be God's people. The New Testament describes circumcision as a sign and a seal of righteousness and faith (Romans 4:11).

Next let us consider *the mark of obedience* to God's commandments. *Whenever people obey God's Word, they somehow become very conspicuous!* We will mention two distinctive marks of Israel, referring first to *the keeping of the Sabbath.*

Truly my sabbaths shall you keep: for it is a sign between me and you throughout your generations, that you may know that I am the Lord who sanctifies you....

So the children of Israel shall keep the sabbath, to observe the sabbath throughout their generations, for a perpetual covenant.

It is a sign between me and the children of Israel forever....

Exodus 31:13,16,17

Similarly, *the keeping of Passover* is called "a *sign*, a memorial, a token," and "frontlets between the eyes," which is a visible reminder. (See Exodus 13:9,16.)

It is no accident that the Hebrew word for "sign" in this scripture is the same word that is used for the "mark" which God put upon Cain! The word is *oth*, which means "a signal, a flag or beacon, monument, evidence, mark, sign, token," and so forth. (We discussed the word *oth* in the chapter on the letter *nun*.)

The particular holy days which God gave to Israel "marked" them as a people.

Now let us briefly consider God's repeated declarations that He has separated Israel from other peoples, made His heritage a sanctified people unto Himself, and set them apart from other nations. This fact is emphasized in scripture and is proved again by history.

Have you ever considered what a separating effect the Law has had on Israel's distinctness? Beginning with his circumcision on the eighth day after birth, and continuing through his life, the Jewish person is unique. He or she has different clothing, different forms of worship, eats different foods, and, if Hebrew speaking, communicates in a different language from that of all other people.

All this, along with the great spiritual riches which God bestowed upon the Hebrew nation, has prompted someone to make this very true observation: *"The Jew is the most God-marked man upon Earth."*

The signs or marks of God's people do not stop with the externals which we have just recounted, important though the Lord declared them to be. But He also spoke of the need for a "circumcision of the heart." (Please read Deuteronomy 30:6; Jeremiah 4:4; 9:25,26.)

The scripture maintains that a true Jew possesses the circumcised heart (Romans 2:28,29). The New Testament as well as the prophecy of Ezekiel show that this circumcision of the heart takes place at water baptism. (See Colossians 2:11,12 and Ezekiel 36:25-27.) The circumcised heart is a mark of a believer.

Another mark of a true follower of Jesus is to practice genuine love and compassion. Jesus said, "By this shall all men know that you are my disciples, *if* you have love one to another" (John 13:35). How many professed followers of Jesus have this mark?

We also ponder the following question: How many people have endured persecution for His sake; persecution which leaves wounds in the physical body? Paul endured such treatment, and he said, "From now on, let no one trouble me: for I carry in my body the marks of the Lord Jesus" (Galatians 6:17).

It is fitting to state at this point that the Bible speaks of marks and signs of God's ownership of His people, yet most of these do not have to do with a physical marking. In fact, the Law strictly prohibits anyone from making any "cuttings in the flesh, or printing any marks" upon themselves (Leviticus 19:28).

One exception was allowed in piercing the ear of a lifelong servant to denote that he voluntarily wished to belong to his master (Deuteronomy 15:17).

As far as the mark of circumcision is concerned, it is not a scar or a disfigurement, but as reason, science, and hygiene confirm, a betterment. How different the Israelites were from pagan societies whose citizens cut, mutilated, gouged, pierced, and painted their bodies!

Not only did primitive societies degrade themselves through unholy marking, but the most evil and satanic regime mentioned in the Bible will force all its citizens to receive "a mark in their right hand, or in their foreheads," an evil mark that pertains to the beast (Revelation 13:16,17).

This mark will identify and unite all who hate God. It is *the mark of slavery* to the evil which will totally degrade and destroy every individual who submits to it. But the marks of God's covenant, which we are continuing to study, are marks of freedom, dignity, and righteousness. May God be praised!

The mark of God is a mark of protection. In Revelation 9:4, we read of a tormenting plague which will befall the whole human race — and only those who have "the seal of God in their foreheads" will be spared!

This is reminiscent of the reference in Ezekiel 9:4-6, where the letter *tav* was marked on the foreheads of the men whom God intended to spare in the slaughter that befell Jerusalem. God commanded the avenging angels to slay all that they found in the Holy City, with this exception: "but come not near any man upon whom is the mark; and begin at my sanctuary."

This powerful verse shows that even in Jerusalem, and even at the Temple itself, there were few people who were living in true covenant relationship with God.

Tav, the mark of the covenant, saved the lives of the faithful — those who, as verse 4 states, lamented and grieved over the sins of Jerusalem. *What a statement of the value God places on the ministry of intercession!*

While we are speaking of the mark of protection, we shall make one last comment about the sign that God appointed for Cain. This mark was, as *Torah* commentator W. G. Plaut has said, "not a brand of rejection, but a sign of protection against blood revenge."

The *Midrash (Berashis Rabbah* 22:13) relates the following story. After the Lord had appointed a mark for Cain, Adam met him and asked, "How did your case go?"

Cain declared, "I repented and am reconciled."

Upon hearing this, Adam began to strike himself, crying, "So great is the power of repentance, and I did not know it!"

By consulting any of the charts which document the development of Hebrew script, one can see that *tav* was written as a cross shape during the Old and New Testament periods. First it looked like a cross or "plus" sign; then like the letter "x." In modern script, the lower left corner acquired a foot or stem, and the other arms were squared out to form a right angle.

Why was this letter in the shape of a cross? *What does a cross-shaped mark represent?* It normally brings to mind one of two things. First, of course, it represents the cross upon which Jesus died. Second, it suggests the oldest and most primitive mark or signature of one's name — a custom which has been in existence for thousands of years. Many cultures knew of an x-shaped mark used in the signing of documents. (*Tav* the mark.)

The history of crosses and crucifixion is surprising. Crucifixion was first a Persian means of execution. When the Roman Empire overtook Persia, the Romans discovered crucifixion and considered it the cruelest form of punishment in existence. It says something about the Roman psyche when we discover that the Romans immediately implemented this cruel Persian torture as an acceptable means of punishment.

It has been remarked that stoning was the prescribed means of execution in the Law of Moses and that crucifixion was of foreign origin. This is true, yet the Lord specifically prepared the understanding of Israel in Moses' day for the time when crucifixion would be commonplace and instructed them to bury without delay anyone who was hung on a tree.

This insured that the scriptures concerning the death, burial, and resurrection of His Son — the expected Deliverer — would be properly fulfilled. The scripture in question is Deuteronomy 21:22,23:

> **If a man has committed a sin worthy of death, and he is put to death, and you hang him on a tree,**
>
> **his body shall not remain all night upon the tree, but you shall in all cases bury him that day (for he that is hanged is accursed of God), that your land is not defiled.**

Of course, Jesus was innocent of any sin, but since He was considered to be guilty and was put on the tree, He fulfilled this verse, as it plainly states in Galatians 3:13: "The

Messiah has redeemed us from the curse of the Law, being made a curse *for us:* for it is written, Cursed is everyone that is hanged upon a tree."

The part about the immediate burial of persons slain in this manner was fulfilled in John 19:38-42. Two very important Jewish religious officials who had become friends of Jesus were the ones who saw that He had a dignified, expensive, proper Jewish burial.

The first man was Joseph of Arimathaea, a member of the *Sanhedrin,* the supreme Jewish court, which had determined that Jesus should die. In Mark and Luke we find that Joseph was an honorable counselor, a good and just man who had not agreed with the counsel and deed of the Sanhedrin concerning Jesus.

Joseph was a rich man who buried Jesus in his own tomb, thus fulfilling Isaiah 53:9, which says of the suffering Messiah, "He made his grave with the rich in his death."

The other man was Nicodemus, also a member of the ruling Jewish council. He provided nearly one hundred pounds of expensive spices for the burial. According to John 19:40, these two men wrapped Jesus' body in the linen with the spices and buried Him.

It is seldom noticed that it was not His family, His many disciples, or even His twelve apostles who lovingly and carefully prepared Jesus' body for burial; rather, it was two wealthy and influential Jewish religious officials, both of them Pharisees, whose kindness to Jesus was shown through this deed.

Tav is the final letter of the Hebrew alphabet. This shows that the sacrifice of Jesus is the final means of Redemption for Jew and Gentile, for Israel, and for all the world. It is God's final means for bringing us into covenant with Himself.

Tav finds its ultimate fulfillment in the very thing its shape reveals — the means of Jesus' death, which reconciles us to God!

It is precisely in this crucifixion of the Messiah that the mystery of the ages is revealed. In His sacrificial death, whereby He, by the grace of God, was permitted to taste death for every man (Hebrews 2:9), God's Messiah took the sin and penalty for the whole world upon Himself. He opened the New Covenant, which *marks* us as ones who belong to God.

Tav, therefore, is a mark of our protection. The mark of the covenant declares to all that we are the Lord's own sheep — His redeemed people.

We belong to Him because He purchased us in His own blood!

Epilogue

By David Michael

*I*t is no accident that Hebrew should have for its first letter a sacrificial animal and for its last letter a cross.

Most certainly God intended that this alphabet should communicate to the Hebrew nation ideas concerning His plan of Redemption, His nature, His typology, and, above all, His Messiah.

In this book, every letter has simply been related to scriptures which incontrovertibly speak about Jesus. Six of the letters are actual names of Jesus in scripture: Temple, burden-bearer, door, nail, water, and head. Six of the letters concern His ministry: window, weapon, fence, teacher, support, and fishhook.

Another six letters represent His physical features, which the Bible emphasizes as being of great importance: hand, arm (wing), eye, mouth, neck, and tooth. Three letters have to do with His sacrificial death: sacrifice, serpent, and cross. And one letter, *nun*, has to do with His Resurrection.

This is a total of 22 letters, which is the entire alphabet. The *whole* alphabet introduces the Messiah — His person, names, ministry, death, and Resurrection. Above all are *aleph* and *tav*, the beginning and the ending of God's message through Israel to the world.

In closing, we mention one final fact about *aleph* and *tav*, the first and last letters of the Hebrew alphabet. When placed together, they make the Hebrew word *et*, spelled *aleph tav*. It is a word that is not translatable into English. It simply shows that an active verb is about to receive its direct object.

The word occurs many hundreds of times in the Bible. For example, it occurs two times in the first verse of Genesis: "In the beginning God created [et] the heaven and [et] the earth." Because this word appears to be merely a peculiarity of grammatical structure, it has received little attention. But in Zechariah 12:10 we read, "And they shall look upon me [et] they have pierced...."

In order for this scripture to make sense in the English language, the translators provided the pronoun "whom" in the place of the word *et.* In English it reads, "they shall look upon me *whom* they have pierced," which means the same as the concise Hebrew words "they shall look upon me they pierced."

Who is this "whom" that was pierced? He is the *alpha-tav (et)* that fits directly *between* "me" and "they": "and they shall look upon ME *et* THEY have pierced." *Here is the one intermediary between God and man — pierced to bring them together!*

How do we know that *aleph-tav* is the name of Jesus? It is because He Himself said so! Revelation 1:11 in the Hebrew New Testament says, "I am the *Aleph* and the *Tav"*; that is to say, the *sacrifice* of the *cross,* AND the pierced one of Zechariah 12:10!

Jesus is the Aleph and the Tav, the First and the Last, the A through Z of God's plan of Redemption!

"Messiah's Portrait"

By David Michael

Aleph is the gentle ox
for work and sacrifice;
Beth is the House of God
to which we turn our eyes.

Gimel is the burdened one
who carried our griefs away;
Daleth is the open door —
the Lord's flock need not stray.

He is the open window
through which God's world we see;
Vav is that hook or nail
which holds so faithfully.

Zayin is God's mighty sword
that makes and keeps us free;
it is His everlasting Word
which endures eternally.

Cheth is our strong defense,
security it will give;
Teth is the suspended one
to which we look and live.

Yod is God's gentle hand
which guides us from the start;
Kaph is Messiah's wings
which hold us near His heart.

Lamed is that special goad
which teaches us His ways;
Mem is the life-producing water
that satisfies always.

Nun is a fish, the sign
that shows who lives again;
Samech is the loving support of
mankind's truest friend.

Ayin is Messiah's eyes
which knew uncounted tears;
Pey is the mouth of the Lord
which speaks calm to our fears.

Tzaddi, a trusty fishhook
to draw His people out;
Qoph, the circle that gives the ax
the necessary clout.

Resh is the chief among ten thousand,
higher than kings of the Earth;
rejected in His generation
but possessing eternal worth.

Shin, those perfect fleece-like teeth
convey what firmness is;
and *Tav*, the mark of the covenant —
the Lord knows who are His.

There is a priceless treasure
in this Hebrew alphabet —
and though it's very simple,
many have not found it yet.

From *Aleph* down to *Tav* it is
a portrait that we find;
Messiah's introduction, which
God alone designed.

These twenty-two simple letters,
which children recite and sing,
reveal Jesus the Messiah,
Israel's glorious King.

Selected Bibliography

A. Judaica

Midrash Rabbah, Genesis. Volume 1 translated by Rabbi Dr. H. Freedman, B.A., Ph.D. London, New York: The Soncino Press, 1983.

The Pentateuch and Rashi's Commentary, Genesis. A linear translation into English by Rabbi Abraham Ben Isaiah and Rabbi Benjamin Sharfman. Brooklyn, New York: S. S. & R. Publishing Company, Inc., 1949.

The Jewish Encyclopedia. Prepared by more than four hundred scholars and specialists. Isidore Singer, Ph.D., projector and managing editor. Twelve volumes. New York and London: Funk and Wagnalls Company, 1901.

The Torah. A modern commentary. New York: Union of American Hebrew Congregations, 1981.

Bereishis — Genesis. A new translation with a commentary anthologized from Talmudic, Midrashic, and rabbinic sources. Brooklyn, New York: Mesorah Publications, Ltd., 1977.

Ramban (Nachmanides). Commentary on the Torah, Genesis. Translated and annotated with index by Rabbi Dr. Charles B. Chavel, Ph.B., M.A., LL.B., D.H.L., D.D. New York, New York: Shilo Publishing House, Inc., 1971.

Rashi on the Pentateuch, Genesis. Translated and annotated by James H. Lowe. London: The Hebrew Compendium Publishing Company (J. Lowe), 1928.

The Wisdom in the Hebrew Alphabet. By Rabbi Michael L. Munk. Overview by Rabbi Nosson Scherman. Mesorah Publications, Ltd., 1983. Permission to quote has been requested.

B. Bible Translations

The Bible, King James Version. Many publishers, various editions. 1611.

The Amplified Bible. Grand Rapids, Michigan: Zondervan Publishing House, 1965.

The Holy Bible, New International Version. New York: American Bible Society, 1978.

The Interlinear Bible, Hebrew/English. Jay P. Green, Sr., general editor and translator. Grand Rapids, Michigan: Baker Book House, 1976.

Ha-Brit Ha-Chadashah. Hebrew New Testament. Jerusalem: Yanetz Ltd., 1976.

The Holy Scriptures – A New Translation. According to the traditional Hebrew text the Jewish Publication Society of America, Philadelphia, Pennsylvania 1960 Originally three volumes; Torah, Prophets, Writings, now in one volume.

The Holy Scriptures According to the Masoretic Text. The Jewish Publication Society of America, Philadelphia, Pennsylvania 1917.

C. Lexicons and Dictionaries

Gesenius' Hebrew and Chaldee Lexicon. By Samuel Prideaux Tregelles, LL.D. Grand Rapids, Michigan: Wm. B. Eerdmans Publishing Company, reprint 1949.

Old Testament Word Studies. By William Wilson. Grand Rapids, Michigan: Kregel Publications, 1978.

Hebrew English Lexicon of the Bible, Schocken Books First Paperback Edition 1975 New York, NY.

Hebrew and Chaldee Dictionary to the Old Testament, compiled by Alexander Harkavy. Hebrew Publishing Co. New York, New York 1914.

Theological Word Book of the Old Testament by Harris - Archer and Waltke. Two volumes. Moody Press, Chicago, Illinois 1980.

Theological Dictionary of the Old Testament by Botterweck Eerdmans Publishing Company Grand Rapids, Michigan. Seven volumes available, more will be forthcoming 1974.

D. Commentaries

Acres of Rubies. By LeBaron W. Kinney. New York: Loizeaux Brothers, Inc., 1942.

Christ in the Hebrew Alphabet. By John MacMillan. London, Edinburgh: Marshall Brothers Limited, circa 1940.

The Alphabet of God. By John Montgomerie. Iverness: R. Jeans, Ravenston, 1940.

Hebrew Honey. Volumes 1 and 2. By Al Novak. New York: Vantage Press, 1965.

E. Encyclopedias

Wycliffe Bible Encyclopedia. Editors: Charles F. Pfeiffer, B.D., Th.M., Ph.D.; Howard F. Vos, Th.M., M.A., Th.D., Ph.D.; John Rae, B.D., Th.M., M.A., Th.D. Chicago: Moody Press, 1975.

The Zondervan Pictorial Encyclopedia of the Bible. General editor, Merrill C. Tenney. Grand Rapids, Michigan: Zondervan Publishing House, 1975.

The Interpreter's Dictionary of the Bible. New York, Nashville: Abingdon Press, 1962.

Cyclopaedia of Biblical, Theological, and Ecclesiastical Literature. By the Rev. John McClintock, D.D., and James Strong, S.T.D. Grand Rapids, Michigan: Baker Book House, reprint 1968.

Dictionary of the Bible Editor James Hastings. Five volumes. T. and T. Clark Edinburgh, Scotland 1895.

Dick Mills, the father of David Michael, has a background in biblical vocabulary and the etymology of Bible words. He wrote Greek and Hebrew word studies in the 1970s for Ward Chandler's *Preacher's Homiletic Magazine* and for the now discontinued *Logos* magazine. In the 1980s, he wrote Greek word studies for the British *Renewal* magazine.

In the 1990s, he compiled the Greek "Word Wealth" studies in Thomas Nelson's *Spirit-filled Life Bible,* edited by Jack Hayford. He also did the Greek word studies for *The Spirit-filled Believer's Topical Bible,* produced by Harrison House. Dick and David completed the preliminary work on Strong's coding for two books published by Kregel Publications: Alfred Jones' *Dictionary of O. T. Proper Names* and W. Wilson's *O. T. Word Studies.*

In addition to an active traveling ministry, Dick researches Bible words by special assignment for authors, publishers, seminaries, and schools of the Bible.

Dick and his faithful wife, Betty, have been married for 37 years, residing all that time in Hemet, California. Dick and Betty have been blessed with two children, David and Deborah, and seven grandchildren.